Thomas Henry Lister

Hulse House

Vol. I

Thomas Henry Lister

Hulse House
Vol. I

ISBN/EAN: 9783337051716

Printed in Europe, USA, Canada, Australia, Japan

Cover: Foto ©ninafisch / pixelio.de

More available books at **www.hansebooks.com**

HULSE HOUSE.

A Novel.

By the Author of "Anne Grey."

IN TWO VOLUMES.

VOL. I.

London:
Saunders, Otley, and Co., Conduit Street.
1860.

LONDON
F. SHOBERL, PRINTER, 37, DEAN STREET, SOHO, W.

HULSE HOUSE.

CHAPTER I.

THE story I am going to tell happened about thirty years ago. It was before railways traversed our country in all directions, before coaches were robbed of their four-in-hand glories, before penny postage deprived the M.P. of his exclusive privilege. My two sisters, Martha and Jane, have a tender recollection of the good old abuses that flourished in our youth. They shake their heads at one another, as they see the young girls walking boldly up the village road with their small hats and short petticoats, and men-like jackets, speaking dictatorially to their papas and mammas, and composedly returning the stare of the young men. But I only laugh: manners and customs change; our sense of propriety and our good taste are shocked, but new virtues come in with new vices—these girls are active and energetic; they will not be loved and respected as their modest grandmothers were, but they rouse and amuse, and they do a great deal of hard bodily and mental work. They make a good appearance on the stage of life, and all England is now a stage, and there is no quiet nook left in our island in which violets may blush unseen, and we begin to wonder what the poet meant.

But I am not wishing to speak of the present. I am going back to about thirty years ago, when I was riding through a quiet, pretty village in the north of England. The road on one side was bounded by a very high wall, which shut out a large wooded park from the street-like village. I felt sad as I looked at the grand, massy groups of forest trees in the park, and just saw the old gray chimneys of the large, gloomy house, rising above the grove that surrounded it. I had no reason for the feeling, that I could define, and I can only imagine it prophetical. Perhaps it was one of those sensations which are now called mesmeric influences!

When I reached the inn, and stopped to bait my horse, I was told that this high wall had been built by the present owner, who, though young,

rich, and handsome, had completely shut himself
out from society. My curiosity was aroused. I
asked many questions, and gained some information
about the mysterious tenant of the gloomy
house. In after times, circumstances brought me
acquainted with many particulars of his history,
and of those connected with it. I tried to write
down what I had gleaned, and I now give the
story as it came out of my workshop. I have a
warm interest in some of the characters. I fancy
myself behind the scenes as to their thoughts and
feelings, and I have written down what I suppose
they might have been, touching them, perhaps,
with the colouring of my own habits of thought
and opinion, but leaving them as much as possible
in the hues with which their own individual characters
invested them.

I begin, then, about thirty years ago. The drawing-room
at Hulse Parsonage is bright with the
sunshine of a spring day. Lucy Crofton is sitting
there; she raises her head every now and then to
look at the scene out of doors, whilst a half-smile
plays round her mouth, telling of her deep enjoyment
of the beauty that meets her eyes. It is a
gay spring garden of tulips, hyacinths, and anemonies,
with a background of dark green shrubs
in parts and the more aerial background of blue

hills and distant woods in others, and the intermediate interest of a gleaming river, large handsome forest trees, and budding hedgerows, in pleasing confusion of lines. All these combined, make up a view of great beauty from the bay window in which she is seated.

Lucy Crofton herself harmonizes well with the softness of the out-door view. She is pretty, graceful, and quiet; but her head is raised at times with quick animation, and her eyes lighten up with humour and intelligence.

The door opens; there is a bustle and a clatter in the room—Lucy's sister-in-law, Mrs. Walter Crofton, has entered. She is handsome, and well dressed, but she does not amalgamate well with the flowers, and the landscape, and with Lucy Crofton. There is neither repose nor grace about her. She gives a sharp look at Lucy, as if ready to find fault if she could discover a reason for it: she makes a few remarks, and then bustles out of the room again, and Lucy is left to her drawing, and to the contemplation of the red and yellow tulips, as the sun's slanting rays catch each in turn, and gild them with new beauty; but a little shade rests for a moment on her face, and then it resumes its usual placidity.

Before I really begin my story, I must tell the

reader that Mrs. Walter Crofton was no other than Miss Eliza Layton, the belle of that very sociable country neighbourhood near D——, of which, no doubt, as Miss Eliza Layton thinks every one must have heard. When she first knew Walter Crofton, he was only a curate, with a small income; but in consideration of his being the eldest son of a country gentleman of some fortune, she kindly allowed him to fall in love with her, although he was some years her junior. This act of generous condescension on her part was caused, as she owned, by her pity for the poor young clergyman, who was so simple-minded and abstracted, in spite of his great abilities, that he sadly wanted the fostering care of a shrewd, active wife; and from this praiseworthy inducement she consented to marry him on his succeeding to a very good family living.

Walter's agreeable, gentleman-like father was much petted and patronised by the smart, handsome Mrs. Walter, and the family place was looked after by her with the most benevolent interference with every one's comfort; but, alas! Mrs. Walter's care was thrown away! Old Mr. Crofton had had an extravagant brother, and Walter found at his father's death that the fortune was only half what was expected, and that the family place must be sold. His only brother, Edward, was already launched in the world with a government appointment, but for his little sister Lucy, who was about fifteen years younger, he must himself provide.

Walter let life slip too easily by: he did not try to check Mrs. Walter's many faults and failings, but he was firm when roused by affection or a sense of duty. This was the case when, after his father's death, he brought Lucy to their home. Mrs. Walter cried, sulked, and did all that a sensible woman was capable of, to change a kind-hearted husband's determination, but Walter was not to be moved. Mrs. Walter then showed her good sense by ceasing to oppose. She only talked with unusual energy about economy, and kept a quick eye on her sister-in-law's failings, whilst Walter subsided peacefully into his arm-chair, his studies, and his clerical duties, which in a large, populous, and much scattered parish, kept him in constant employment.

I never quite made out why Walter Crofton married Eliza Layton. Perhaps if we look at half the elderly married couples in the world, we should be equally puzzled for a reason why they ever came together. All I can say of Walter Crofton is, that he hated trouble, except for the good of others; he was very kind-hearted, and perfectly unsuspicious of guile; Miss Eliza Layton's attentions had been untiring—she insinuated that her heart might break if he looked coldly on her, and so it ended in Miss Eliza becoming Mrs. Walter Crofton. Besides having a very kind, easy husband, Mrs. Walter possessed two other comforts—she had a grievance, and she had something to wish for—and few of us are very happy unless we possess one or other of these blessings. The orphan sister was sadly mild for a grievance, but the wish for more society was delightfully strong.

"I am used to a good sociable neighbourhood," was her frequent remark. "Dinner invitations at least twice a week! Archeries, county balls, and a friendly chat with four or five families at the church door every Sunday; and here we are quite in a desert! Worse than all, Hulse House without a tenant! I am sure, Walter, if you exerted yourself a little, Hulse House would be taken. A large house, a fine park, a good garden, a range of hot-houses, stabling for twenty horses!—and there is actually no one there! The very hot-houses decaying for want of use! I think I could bear it better if we could buy vegetables from the garden. Such parties as there might be! A pleasant man and his wife, with sons and daughters—companions for poor Lucy. And I always think a great deal more of Lucy than of myself; not that she seems to be aware of it. And, Walter, if I might suggest to you......" Here she looked up. "Oh!" was her exclamation, as she found that Walter had quietly slipped away.

But at length Mrs. Walter was able to utter the following animated exclamation to her husband, "Mr. Crofton, Hulse House is taken!"

"Indeed!" was the quiet reply; with an abstracted look from his book to his wife, and back again to his book.

Mrs. Walter's raptures were not closed. "Taken, Mr. Crofton! Actually taken on a long lease. A rich, unmarried, young man—an excellent neighbour, you see, for us all. A perfect gentleman, and, no doubt, extremely agreeable. Walter! why will you go on reading that old musty-fusty book, instead of attending to all that I am taking the trouble to say to you; and it is such a very important matter, for poor Lucy and altogether; and indeed, as clergyman of the parish, I should have thought that *you* might have cared a little."

"Oh, certainly!" said Walter, meekly laying down his book. "I am glad Hulse House is taken; and I hope, for your sake, we shall have pleasant neighbours."

"Neighbours!" exclaimed Mrs. Walter. "Have I not been telling you it is a single man?"

"Yes, so you did, I believe," said Walter; "but"—rousing himself a little—"but he may marry some day."

Mrs. Walter smiled, and was mollified. "Yes, Walter, you are quite right; he *may* marry some day. He will have several very eligible neighbours; and, for his own sake, I only hope he may choose wisely."

"I hope so," said Walter, and his eyes were again on his book.

"Yes; and, of course, Walter, you will call on him directly."

The book was despondingly relinquished; it was time to take up the subject. "We shall see," he said, "whether I can be of any use to him. If he is rich, healthy, and happy, perhaps he would not receive my visits very warmly."

"Nonsense, Mr. Crofton! why will you always lower yourself into being only the country clergyman, instead of the country gentleman as you are? You must call, of course, as an equal. I did not marry you, to be only asked to dinner as the parson's wife; used as I had been, before I married, to be asked out to dinner, two or three, or even four times a week, and at archery meetings always placed at the best targets—Lord Cramwell picking up my arrows, and Mr. Fotheringay making a point of taking me in to dinner."

Walter was now deep in his book; Mrs. Walter shook her head, and hurried away to find a better listener. She found Lucy.

" Lucy, here is excellent news!" she exclaimed. Lucy looked up, pleased and wondering. " Hulse House is taken! My dear Lucy, I am quite rejoiced on your acccount; as to myself, I never care how much or how little society I have!" Lucy's look of pleasure had subsided, but she smiled. " A rich young man," Mrs. Walter continued; " and you see, Lucy, as he is unmarried,"—she checked herself—" that is, my dear Lucy, he will be a pleasant addition, as you have no young companions excepting Barker Preston, and one cannot call him a very eligible one."

Whether eligible or not, Mr. Barker Preston was often at the Parsonage. He was the eldest son of a poor baronet. When he could neither hunt nor shoot, he found the Parsonage a pleasant lounge; and, as he was simple-minded and goodhearted, Lucy was always glad to see him. Nor did she undervalue the heartiness of his applause after each of her songs, nor despise his unfailing admiration of her drawings, whether looked at upside down or not.

"Well, Mrs. Crofton," he exclaimed one morning as he came into the drawing-room where Mrs. Walter and Lucy were sitting together, "well, Mrs. Crofton, such news! I hope you have not heard it, for I wished to be the first to tell you. Miss Crofton, can you guess what it is?"

"Oh, pray tell us at once," said Mrs. Crofton, "I hate guessing! What is it?"

"I bet anything you'll neither of you ever find it out!" said Barker Preston, laughing heartily.

"Why then," said Lucy, "you had better tell us at once."

"Ah, Miss Crofton," said Barker Preston, clapping his hands with delight; "that's just like you, so clever! as you always are."

Mrs. Crofton became more impatient. "Is it about Hulse House?" she said, eagerly.

"That's the best guess I ever heard!" exclaimed Barker Preston, "and so I will tell you all about it. You heard Hulse House was taken? Well, the fellow's come!"

"Is he, really?" said Mrs. Crofton.

"Yes, and what do you suppose—here it is— I think I shall surprise you!" and he drew a card out of his pocket. "Here it is—now just listen: 'Mr. Colville' (that's his name you know), 'Mr. Colville presents his compliments to Sir George and Mr. Preston, and whilst he thanks them for their obliging attention, he takes the opportunity of stating that, as he wishes to live in complete seclusion, he can neither receive nor return the visits of Sir George and Mr. Preston, or any of his neighbours who may kindly honour him by the intention of calling upon him.' And then he dates it 'Hulse House, the 20th.' Odd! isn't it?"

"This is a joke, Mr. Preston," said Mrs. Walter, angrily, her face growing very red.

"Joke, to be sure! By Jove, if it is not the best joke I have heard for a long time!" was the reply. "A fellow coming to take a capital house in the neighbourhood, setting us all in a blaze of excitement, and then to have him sending out a card like this! I think it is the best joke I ever heard."

"But you don't mean it's true that he really sent this card?" said Mrs. Crofton still more annoyed.

"Not send this card—but I do, indeed."

"Well, then," said Mrs. Crofton, indignantly, "I must say that I think it a most unjustifiable thing! a house of that kind to be shut up by a gloomy, mad misanthrope! I should say it was a public nuisance, and I have no doubt he will be indicted as such; or, if he is not, I am quite sure he ought to be! It will be impossible that we can ever walk out again for fear of meeting him, for how could we answer for our lives in one of his paroxysms! I should say, decidedly, that whoever let him that house, ought to be fined." And Mrs. Crofton stopped, too much hurried and excited to say more.

"Oh! bless you," said Preston, "he is as sane as I am; you need not frighten yourself. And as to your meeting him, there's no fear of that, for he has ordered a high wall to be built outside the park, and his groom says he never means to stir beyond it."

"Oh, he has a groom then?" said Mrs. Crofton.

"Yes, and a fine stud of horses, and two capital hunters."

"But what did the groom say?" asked Mrs. Crofton, eagerly.

"That his master did not like much talking, and generally wrote down his orders."

"Did he say he was mad?" said Mrs. Crofton, bitterly.

"Not a bit, but a thorough gentleman, only queer."

"Poor man!" said Lucy, "he must be unhappy."

"Ay, I thought you would pity him!" said Mr. Preston, looking benignly at Lucy; "your kind heart you know! And the groom says he believes that he's had some great sorrow, and so he made a vow never to speak to any one again; and hearing of Hulse, and what a dull neighbourhood it was, he thought it would exactly suit him to live and die in."

"A most absurd story," exclaimed Mrs. Walter. "We shall see how long he will keep his vow!"

"Yes, we shall see!" said Mr. Preston.

"And then the idea of coming here to be quiet!" said Mrs Walter

"Ay, indeed!" said Barker Preston, giving a side glance at her.

The excitement about Mr. Colville continued to be very active in Hulse for some time. If much was said that was untrue, it was quite certain that the lodge gates were locked, and that the lodge keepers refused admittance to any one but on business as labourers or tradesmen; and that when Walter Crofton asked at the lodge whether Mr. Colville would see him, a card was put into his hand similar in purport to that Barker Preston had shown to Mrs. Crofton. Great anxiety was felt as to the effect of a Sunday on Mr. Colville; would he or would he not appear at church? During half the service, Mrs. Crofton's eyes constantly wandered to the still empty pew belonging to Hulse House. But, alas! it was never filled with any object more interesting than the old red cushions that rested in a row round the seat. Mr. Colville, for one Sunday, at least, had no inclination for church. In the bitterness of her disappointment, Mrs. Crofton declared her conviction that he was either a Jew or an Atheist. The only compensation was in seeing a very respectable, staid-looking man, between thirty and forty years of age, in the pew assigned to the Hulse House servants, and in ascertaining, after church, that he was Mr. Colville's valet and butler, and that his name was Hodson.

CHAPTER II.

There was a strong contrast between that old gray Manor House at Hulse, in which the recluse had chosen to immure himself, and that small white-washed, staring house, which catches all the sun, and has its door open to all the world, and its neat little garden glaring forth with the brightest of flowers to every passer-by in the village of Hulse.

" Come in, my dear, come in, and don't stay pottering at the door," said a sharp, brisk voice from the very clean, white-papered, white-chintzed sitting-room in Woodbine Cottage, as Lucy Crofton lingered for a moment to look at the flowers. " I hate people staying at the door when once they are announced," went on the voice muttering half to itself. " It's like breaking the seal of a letter, and then putting it by before you've read it. Let me know the worst at once ! Come in, Lucy," was said aloud as Lucy walked in. " Come in, and sit down there, child, where I can see your face as I talk to you. I don't like speaking to a thing I can't see. Your face is not such an ugly one that you need hide it. Not that I care for a pretty face—two large eyes and one straight nose, and all the rest of it to match—unless there is some meaning in it. I would as soon look at a sign post."

Miss Walcott stopped a minute, perhaps to take breath, but, meantime, she looked at the very large book she had been reading when Lucy came in, peering at the page with her spectacles and then putting a mark at the place where she stopped.

Whilst she pauses, we may as well mention that Miss Walcott, or Mrs. Mary Walcott as she ought to be called, is a little brisk-looking old lady, with very sharp black eyes, and thin lips, and a rather large aquiline nose. She has a clear, pale complexion; she wears a black silk gown, and a black silk shawl pinned over it, and a very clean white concoction of a cap perched on the top of a black wig. She looks as if neither age nor care could depress her, and as if the sparkle of spirit within must keep her up under any circumstances. If hand and foot could not move, we feel quite certain that those piercing black eyes would be moving about everywhere and searching out everything. She never leaves her home, but she is neither dull nor dozy. There is an acute but a very pleasant expression in her face. She looks through you and into you, and she would not spare your foibles, but you are certain she would see all your merits too, though she might seem to scoff at them, and you know that she thinks most affectionately and benignly both of them and of you.

And now having closed her Greek author (for Miss Walcott was a deeply learned little woman), she was off again; talking fast, but so distinctly and precisely, that not a word was lost of that large flow of them that were always ready for all comers.

"So Mrs. Walter is happy at last, my dear! she has got an owner for Hulse House!"—Miss Walcott laughed—a little short satirical laugh—like the bleating of a very small sheep—"and he's shut himself up in it! She's pleased, I guess! Send her to me, Lucy, and let's talk it over. Never wish heartily for anything in your life—if you do, you will be sure to get it, just in a way you don't like. It is a law of nature. I wanted to taste turtle soup—just to know what the epicures raved about—I had it at last and an alderman cousin with it; I hope never to see turtle soup again. That's a pretty bonnet you've got on, Lucy; you look nicely in it. But don't let us talk of dress: I hate it, it's as bad as gossip: but I'll tell you something to put Mrs. Walter in good-humour. Mr. and Mrs. Digby are come to Digby Manor. You will soon be asked there, my dear! Compensation for Hulse House!" and she chuckled again.

"What do you hear about the Digbys?" asked Lucy.

"That they are London people, child, and that is all; but there is some good in that. Never was there such a mistake as to cry down Londoners! A pack of stuff about being worldly! As if people are not just as worldly, when they look cross if the cook don't dress their chicken to their mind! I should like to know whether it is any better to have your thoughts turned to the stuffing of a goose, than to making yourself pleasant to the greatest people of the age? You don't meet the Duke of Wellington, and Rogers, and Sidney Smith, and Sir Humphry Davy, and so many more I can't take time to name, amongst your own turnip fields, I guess! but in a London rout. But then they talk of Walter Scott and Words-worth, and half-a-dozen more in the country.

Yes, to be sure! but all these people don't stand saying 'how do you do,' to you, in your own meadows, I imagine? And after all, they, every one of them, go to London, and there they meet, and they talk—bless you, how they talk! You will never hear such talk in the country if you burrow about it for a hundred years!" She suddenly broke off to say, with a little chuckle, "Ah! here comes Barker Preston! saw you come in, no doubt!" and this was added half to herself.

We must tell the reader that Miss Walcott's chair was placed so that she could see every one who came to her door.

"Bless the man, what is he bringing?" as Barker Preston came in, carrying a basket of strawberries.

"Strawberries!" exclaimed Miss Walcott, sharply, "what made you bring them to me, and there is Dolly Barnes at Lane-end, lying there sick and feverish with her mouth wide open for fruit and getting none? Here! carry them back, Sally. It's very kind of you, Barker Preston, for all that, but what's the use of pampering up an old thing like me with hot-house strawberries? What do I want but neck of mutton and bread pudding?"

Barker Preston laughed, and took the scolding very amiably. "I thought you would like them," he said.

"Like them, yes! and so I like your good-nature, but I want it to be useful."

"Then I'll carry them to the sick woman for you, shall I?"

Miss Walcott's eyes brightened. "I like that better than the strawberries, Barker Preston," she said with a little satisfied grunt; "but stay, pick out the prettiest and you shall give them to Lucy; and come back as quick as you can, for I want to see you. Like them, yes!" she went on, half to herself, when Barker Preston had run off with his basket; "I like his good heart, but it should be guided with good sense. Bringing hot-house strawberries to me!" she chuckled; "why how could I help being a little sharp with him? Strawberries for me to eat! Very fine ones too! You must eat some to please him, Lucy, when he comes back. A German word would describe him, but I don't know an English one. The Germans put half-a-dozen ideas into one. Your German gets on, my dear? You like it?" and her sharp eyes looked into Lucy's for an answer.

Miss Walcott had taught Lucy German, for this learned little lady was a good German scholar, among her other merits.

But I must not linger any more in the gay, white, sunny cottage, with the chattering little Miss Walcott, although I would rather stay there than visit that large, showy mansion in the neighbourhood, to which all eyes are turned with hope and expectation. Mr. and Mrs. Digby had just inherited the property; they were rich people and Londoners, as Miss Walcott had said. The Croftons were soon invited to Digby Manor, and Mrs. Walter's spirits, which had been much depressed by Mr. Colville's unmannerly seclusion, revived under the graciousness of the Digbys' invitation.

"At any rate," she exclaimed, as they drove there, " we shall have no mad infidels here! Mr. Digby opens his lodge gates to his neighbours as every Christian ought to do. They are really fine London people, but they don't shut themselves up like this trumpery Mr. Colville. Indeed, Mr. Crofton, I think you ought to make a stir to have him removed from your parish. Think of the bad effects on others! We shall have the public-house shutting its doors next."

CHAPTER III.

DIGBY MANOR is a great, large, handsome house, with suites of useless rooms, and a large staircase rambling up the middle of it, in a way to frighten timid housemaids who are left to take care of it when the *fam'ly's away;* and the whole affair has an exotic air about it. The flowers are all from the stove or conservatory; strawberries and peas are only admitted out of season; sturdy, out-of-doors, natural objects are out of place at Digby Manor. Mr. Digby's neat, well-dressed figure, his quiet, self-satisfied air, his small voice, his conventional good breeding, are all of the hot-house type. Mr. and Mrs. Digby's ideas are formed on a model; trained by art and not by nature. Mr. Digby in a smock frock, handling a spade, is an impossibility. But Mr. Digby is rich; he is the great man of the neighbourhood, and Digby Manor is the house *par excellence,* and I would not presume to hint at a preference for broad beans and bacon, for hearty laughter and cordial hospitality with red hands and faces, over the well-bred nonchalance of Mr. and Mrs. Digby's white-handed greeting.

Mrs. Digby was a fashion-hunting woman of society. To her, life was society and society a small clique in London; there was nothing important or interesting beyond this. As Miss Walcott afterwards said of her—

"I believe Mrs. Digby thinks no one could live if they were cut by Lady C——!"

I cannot imagine much interest in two such persons; but there was a halo of fashion about Digby Manor that lent its magic to Mrs. Walter Crofton's feelings. The Digbys looked down on her, but she looked up to them, and to some minds this is a pleasant exercise.

Society had not yet unfolded its charms to Lucy; she was but just seventeen, and had seen nothing of the world. Her sister-in-law's depreciating tone had increased her natural diffidence, and the first greeting of the Digbys was not calculated to raise her spirits or to inspire her with self-confidence.

When she and Mrs. Walter came into the drawing-room before dinner, Mrs. Digby was coldly and carelessly civil, and Mr. Digby took the air of a superior in displaying his fine pictures and rare china to new admirers. Mrs. Walter was ready to admire anything Mr. Digby wished, and to listen with pleased attention to his praises of his own discernment and taste, whilst Lucy felt a disagreeable conflict between her sense of the ridiculous and her annoyance at Mrs. Walter's toadyism.

The guests to-day at Digby Manor were Mr. Spencer, a quietly agreeable elderly man, first cousin to Mr. Digby; his daughter, Agnes Spencer; a gossipping old Lady Wedgeburn; a lively French Count; a good-looking, clever Mr. George Berkeley, and some other young men. As Lucy's shyness had not as yet been rubbed off in society, she was not sorry to be taken in to dinner by a very young Mr. Ashton, as being the least formidable if not the most agreeable person in the room; and it was not till she had answered his flow of questions as to her powers of riding, walking, playing, and drawing, that she discovered that her other neighbour was the clever, satirical-looking Mr. George Berkeley, whom she had determined in her own mind to be the most alarming of the party. However, as he was seated between her and Mrs. Digby, who seemed anxious to engross his attention, she thought he would probably not speak to her, and every fear vanished as a lively conversation began between him and his opposite neighbours, the clever little French Count and Miss Spencer, during which Lucy scarcely knew whether to admire most Miss Spencer's beauty and originality, the little Frenchman's terse, neat sayings, Mr. Berkeley's general agreeableness, grave or gay, or the easy skill, so readily attained by people of the world, with which Mrs. Digby was civilly attended to and passed by if she tried to join in the conversation.

But at length an unguarded smile of Lucy's attracted Mr. Berkeley's attention, and, having once spoken to her, he went on talking so good-naturedly and agreeably that Lucy wondered why she had been afraid of him, until Mrs. Digby's frequent interposition and Mr. Berkeley's answers to some of her remarks reminded her that he was satirical and formidable. She caught his eye resting on her once or twice during the evening, and she in her modesty thought he must be ridiculing her country *gaucherie* of appearance and manner, little knowing what a winning little personage she was, and that it was not very strange for any one to take pleasure in looking at her pretty intelligent countenance.

Lucy was lamentably deficient in vanity. She never considered whether her countenance was pretty or not, but she suffered under that youthful sensation of shyness which, thirty years ago, was not uncommon to young ladies on first appearing in society, but which has since become obsolete in consequence of the superior knowledge of the world and of their own merits which they now are happy enough to possess.

Lucy had inherited from her father a love of the study of character, but amongst the present set of new acquaintance the only two who excited much of this kind of interest were Miss Spencer and Mr. George Berkeley. Of the others, Mr. Spencer was a person to like and love, as agreeable, kind, and gentlemanlike; but there were no mysteries to be unveiled—Lucy could imagine no hidden romance in his life or character, any more than she could in that of the lively French Count.

The Comte de V——, it was true, was delightful in society—he was certain to prevent a party from being dull, but that was all!—Lucy could not care to speculate on his thoughts and feelings.

Not so with Miss Spencer. Lucy was almost startled at first by the novelty and originality of her character, and she could have listened to her and watched her for ever. Sometimes her admiration ran high, and then it was chilled as she observed a slight want of softness, a careless defiance of opinion, a haughty determination to talk to none but the pleasantest people in the room; but her beauty and agreeableness soon won back Lucy's admiration, and mixed with this there was the interest of trying to solve the mystery of a strangely sad look that came over her countenance very suddenly in the midst of her gaiety. Lucy would have thought her unhappy, till in the next moment her wonderfully clear, merry, ringing laugh sounded in her ears, and she saw her bright face beaming with animation as she raised her head with a little wilful toss, as if in the firmness of proud self-reliance and youthful gaiety and vigour of spirit.

As to Mr. George Berkeley, I will not say that it was exactly his good looks, the peculiarly fascinating tones of his voice, the softness and earnestness that often dwelt in his eyes, which interested Lucy, but rather his extreme agreeableness, and the sort of uncertainty raised in her mind as to what his opinions would be on the next subject spoken of—some fear of his ridicule—some doubt of his goodnature—and no doubt of his abilities.

"You must make acquaintance with my Agnes," said the kind, gentle Mr. Spencer to Lucy, after talking to her for some time. "She is very lively, as you see, but I can assure you she is a very good, affectionate kind of person too, and she never forgets to look after her old papa! To-morrow you shall be formally introduced. You will be sure to like one another."

Lucy could have laughed at the idea that Miss Spencer would ever care to speak to her, but she only thanked Mr. Spencer for his goodnature as she wished him good night. Agnes Spencer had already left the room.

The Croftons had now been two days at Digby Manor. The study of character was becoming more interesting and more reciprocal. Miss Spencer and Mr. Berkeley were alone in the library.

"And what do you think of Lucy Crofton?" Agnes suddenly exclaimed.

"And why do you ask?" was George Berkeley's reply.

"That is evasion, Mr. Berkeley. I asked a plain question and you answer me by asking another."

George Berkeley looked down and smiled. "A plain question!" he said, again looking up. "Do you call that a plain question? What do I think of a person! Consider for a moment what that involves. What I think! Do you mean of her appearance, manner, disposition, situation in life......"

"In short," said Miss Spencer, interrupting him, "you will not answer, and I shall draw my own conclusions."

"Oh!" said Mr. Berkeley, and he smiled rather sarcastically: then looking gravely at Miss Spencer, he said—"Now I will tell you what I think of Miss Crofton. I think her a young lady of about seventeen years of age. I think that her brother is a clergyman. I think that her sister-in-law is......"

"Never mind what," exclaimed Agnes. "Don't punish me any more. You are never serious when I wish you to be."

"But now, seriously, Miss Spencer," said Mr. Berkeley, "speaking of Miss Crofton, it strikes me that she is pretty; don't you think so?"

"That was not said seriously," said Miss Spencer; "nevertheless, I will answer in earnest that I think Miss Crofton the most engaging person I ever saw. I know that I am quite determined to win her to be my friend, and I am sure that if I were a man I should certainly fall desperately in love with her."

"I quite agree with you," said George Berkeley, quietly.

"I know you do," exclaimed Agnes, pettishly, "though that odious smile says you don't;" and then a shade came over her face, as if with a sudden and painful change of thought.

But just then her father appeared; and her face brightened with affection as she hastened towards him, and linked her arm in his.

"Ah! my dear Agnes," he said, as he proudly and fondly patted her cheek, "I have been lost without you! Like an old simpleton, I never feel quite happy unless I am within reach of your chattering; but I could not civilly leave Digby sooner. We have been having a dish of politics."

There is a kind of *bonhommie*, a genial air, a roseate hue, cast over everything and everybody in a large country house. Acquaintances are soon made, often as quickly set aside; but, nevertheless, it is fortunate that these little softening oases should occur amidst the sandy deserts of London society.

Miss Spencer and Mr. Berkeley had already been three days in the same house with Walter and Lucy Crofton, and, unconsciously perhaps, some of the vigour, and freshness, and verdure of country originality had been engrafted on their feelings, whilst no doubt they in return had contributed a rich store of aromatic, highly cultured plants, to adorn these fine natural soils.

"Oh, Miss Crofton," said Agnes Spencer to Lucy, on the morning of that third day, "will you let me hear that little German song again? It has been haunting me ever since you sang it yesterday. I never heard anything so pretty, and I am more convinced than ever that German music is better than Italian—the German touches the heart and mind, the Italian only the heart and senses."

"I shall put in a word for English ballads, if you please," said Mr. Berkeley.

"Yes, yes," said Agnes; "so will I, when Miss Crofton sings us some; but wait till you have heard what she says to us in German, before you talk of anything else."

"Yes," he said, after a little pause, when Lucy's sweet, touching voice, had ceased, "there can be nothing more beautiful than that—and I should like to hear one of our best English ballads under the same advantages."

The atmosphere of the Parsonage was not one of adulation, and praise of late was a rarity to Lucy, so that we cannot wonder if she was rather gratified by the compliments—prettily implied, rather than broadly expressed by Miss Spencer and Mr. Berkeley—which followed her performance of one or two English songs. They had the art of praising well, so as to raise instead of lowering the person whom they praised.

"Who was your master, Miss Crofton?" said Mrs. Digby, who came in from the adjoining room at the sound of music. "Your singing is very pretty," she added, in a patronising way, "is not it?" carelessly turning to Miss Spencer, and without waiting for an answer, she asked for a repetition of the last song, rather more as a command than as a request.

Lucy was about to comply, when Mr. Berkeley said pointedly to her, "You are too good-natured, Miss Crofton. Much as we shall lose by not hearing you, you really must not think of singing again till you are rested."

In a far more civil tone Mrs. Digby immediately said, "Pray don't tire yourself. I hope we shall hear you some other time."

Lucy was not sure whether to be vexed or gratified, so she would not look up to thank Mr. Berkeley, but escaped to the next room, where she sat down to her work, and to a deep cogitation on the difference between good-natured assistance and meddling interference; a philosophical inquiry which never came to a decision, as old Lady Wedgeburn drew a chair near to her before it was finished, and was very anxious to tell Lucy a good many of her own sentiments about her friends and acquaintance in general.

When the evening is closed at a country house, a highly confidential feeling is apt to come over the ladies of the party, and instead of going quietly to bed, they stay in one another's rooms " to talk it all over." I do not pretend to judge either of the pleasure or the profit of this social appendix to the day's amusement. All I know is, that the result of a "'quiet little gossip" which Mrs. Digby inflicted on her cousin, Agnes Spencer, that evening, was a pressing request from Mrs. Digby to the Croftons, next morning, that they should all stay a week longer at Digby Manor.

Walter Crofton was obliged to return to his parish, but Mrs. Walter accepted Mrs. Digby's patronizing invitation with great delight, for herself and Lucy. She took advantage, however, of a quiet interval before the party assembled, to fulfil her sisterly duty to Lucy, by reminding her that it was customary for young ladies of her age to be flattered, and made simpletons of; she hoped Lucy would remember that Miss Spencer would probably never think of her again after she left Digby Manor, and she begged her not to put herself forward to attract Mr. Berkeley's notice. He was a man of the world, and it was the custom for such men to turn people into ridicule, after making a great fuss about them in the country.

After this cheering and friendly harangue, Lucy followed Mrs. Walter into the breakfast-room, and she was so anxious to avoid Mr. Berkeley's future contempt, that she gladly accepted Mr. Spencer's offer of a chair next his own, and was happily talking and laughing with her kind neighbour, when a voice near her almost made her start.

"I have secured a place by you, Miss Crofton," were George Berkeley's words, "though you would not say good morning to me."

With the natural and deplorable thoughtlessness of youth, Lucy had entirely forgotten Mrs. Walter Crofton's prudent advice before the end of breakfast!

"How fortunate for me that Mr. Berkeley found no pleasanter place at liberty!" was her thought. "There certainly never was any one half so agreeable."

"But," said my sister Martha, "he is not the hero, for you have taken care to tell us that he is very satirical, and I never yet heard of a satirical hero."

"Oh," said Jane, "there is always a dangerous

character in the way, and I only hope poor Lucy will beware of him."

"And so do I," was my answer. "But then what will she do for a difficult dilemma?"

"Ah!" said Martha and Jane, simultaneously, "that is to be considered."

"You know that my story is founded on fact," I said, "so that I cannot help it if Lucy falls into trouble."

"Very true," said Martha, "so now let us know what happened next day. Lucy, no doubt, though so young, will have her wits about her."

"Indeed, I hope so," was my reply.

CHAPTER IV.

Soon after my interest was first attracted towards Hulse village and its recluse, in that solitary ride, when the old gray chimneys caught my notice, I heard a great deal of Miss Spencer. I would gladly convey to the reader the impression I received of this winning, fascinating young lady. She had warm affections, brilliant talents, great generosity of mind, and a noble contempt for anything mean or base, but she had a high and ungovernable spirit. She was too careless of opinion, too recklessly bent on the indulgence of her own varying whims, even at the expense of others. If sorrows had visited her, the gay, sparkling beauty was but the more proud, witty, and careless, as if she would toss her head in scorn at the idea of grief or disappointment!

It is difficult to describe her character, and still more so to convey the idea of her appearance and manner. Have you ever looked at a landscape with an extensive view of richly wooded country, on a day of alternating sun and cloud, whilst a fresh pleasant breeze is blowing around you? The changes are so great and rapid, that you try in vain to recall the past beauties of the scene, and every now and then there is such a deep, dark gloom, from a large cloud, that you scarcely believe there has been any sunshine or soft gay beauty at all; but before the chilly feeling has confirmed itself, the cloud is gone—out bursts the sun, and the whole scene is more bewitching than ever. Now this gives some idea of your impressions in watching Miss Spencer, whilst another character dawns upon us, such as I wish you to look at in contrast to hers, and which I, for one, love much more to contemplate. It is like one of those quiet spring mornings, where everything is in cheerful, happy repose, whilst we know that there is life and vigour ready for action, and actually going on under that calm serenity.

Lucy Crofton is my sweet spring morning, and I own that I love it, and feel happy, as many others have done, when I come within that mild, gentle influence. Miss Spencer felt this, too.

"How I wish that some odd accident had made you my cousin or my sister," said she one day, suddenly to Lucy, after having watched her for some time; "for then," she added, "it would be all right and proper that I should love you, and I want to have you for a friend, if you will only try to feel a little interest in me."

Lucy looked up rather surprised, and then said, simply, "That is not a very hard task, I think."

Mr. Berkeley probably shared my partiality for spring mornings, for he happened to look up from his book as Agnes and Lucy continued talking together, after the preliminary sentences that I have just recorded, and he was so much interested in watching Lucy's expression, that his book was cruelly neglected, until Mrs. Digby sailed in, in all the vigour and display of a July day at noon.

She slided into a chair between Agnes and Lucy, and said to the latter, "You really must sing that little French song again to us, Miss Crofton."

" As Mrs. Digby commands music," said Agnes, getting up as she spoke, "let us try that duet together, Miss Crofton," and she was at the instrument in an instant.

" Brava, Agnes Spencer!" thought Mr. Berkeley, and he went to help Lucy to find her songs; and then, after a few half-jesting remarks to Miss Spencer on the impossibility of mistaking German for French music, he returned to his book and his arm-chair.

Friendships and acquaintances are often lightly begun, that have a weighty influence on the whole future life, whether for good or for evil. I have been sometimes doomed to watch these small, careless beginnings ripen into important eras, to those who met with so little thought.

My cheerful, light-hearted heroine has no such grave considerations resting on her mind, as she first makes acquaintance with these agreeable guests at Digby Manor. She knows that very possibly she may never meet them again; but, with her young happy spirit, she lets herself fully enjoy this little interlude in her otherwise monotonous life at the Parsonage. When I say monotonous, I mean simply unvaried, for Lucy neither craved after gaiety and excitement, nor was she dull at home. I cannot say that Mrs. Walter's temper was a constant source of pleasure to her; but her own intelligent mind kept her from *ennui*, and opened to her inexhaustible funds of interest in everything around her. She brought this fresh, well-stored, well-regulated mind into society, and there was healthy animation and pleasure in gaining new ideas and seeing new characters. If a little vein of satire, and a quick sense of the ludicrous, was mixed with her graver and more kindly qualities, I hope she will be forgiven.

There were some fresh arrivals at Digby Manor that day, to add to her stock of knowledge. Mr. Godfrey, one of the Digby Manor *habitués*, arrived. He was a tall, dark young man, who lolled in an arm-chair all evening, talking *sotto voce* to Mrs. Digby, or rather allowing her to talk to him, for he was far too indolent to make conversation for himself. Mr. Fitzgerald was the other guest. He was a person who took the cares and pleasures of life with less indolence, but far more quiet good sense. He had shown his good sense especially with regard to Miss Spencer, whom he had loved from her childhood; but he had wisely abstained from obtruding his affection upon her, for he saw that, although Agnes delighted in his society as a friend, she would have rejected him as a lover: and yet he was the very husband her father would have chosen for her — agreeable, clever, amiable, and rich.

"Indeed!" said my sister Martha, "it was a pity she did not look to her father's wishes, rather than to the indulgence of her own fancies."

"Very true," said I; "it would have saved her a great deal of trouble; but, like other young ladies, she preferred choosing for herself."

The charms of society are a hackneyed topic. Though unable to be more than a listener myself, I must confess to a great partiality for really clever talk. Not learned disquisitions, or serious conversations, or instructive lectures—all excellent in their way—but the highly condensed, sharply pointed, clear, vivid, and sparkling conversation of fashionable society; not frivolous—that is a very different matter—but that neat, well expressed, and easy flow of words and ideas, in which, I believe, none but that one small set in society ever excel. I do not speak of its moral or religious worth, but merely as I would of perfection in any other accomplishment; and I was not surprised at Lucy Crofton's wonder and delight as she listened that evening to the conversation between Miss Spencer, Mr. Fitzgerald, the Comte de V——, and Mr. George Berkeley.

And what, it may be asked, did this satirical Mr. Berkeley think of our quiet little country maiden?

When he had first seen her at Digby Manor, his careless glance had soon passed from her to others who had greater claims on his interest. But two or three days elapsed, and this quiet, shy Miss Crofton had made some observations that forced him to think. She looked very pretty and graceful, and he could not help watching for the changes of expression in her countenance. He became more fascinated as he saw more of her. There were depths he had not imagined. He tried his own powers of agreeableness—grave or gay—and still successfully. He tried still further; expecting, nay—if truth be told—hoping for a failure. If so, he was disappointed; and he became alarmed at his own success, for he was too poor to marry: or, if he married, it must be some one with money—well-born, well-bred, and, above all, in his own set in London, or rather in his mother's set—for all these "*must be's*" applied to his mother.

As he looked at Lucy Crofton they grated uncomfortably on his recollection. How would this end? He did not wish to ask; and when Walter Crofton, after a long conversation, said to him, in his hearty, matter-of-fact way, "I hope we shall meet you again," George Berkely responded, with warmth, "Indeed it will not be my fault if we do not often meet!" and then, as he saw a little smile on Lucy's face, he could not resist going to sit down by her, to try and find out why she smiled.

There was but one day more at Digby Manor! What, then, did it signify how much he talked to her on that last evening? What a mind it was to probe into! What a lovely face to watch! What good it did him to talk with one whose feelings and ideas were so just and right!

"I shall come to Digby Manor again, very soon," he said.

"I am very glad," was Lucy's unguarded answer, followed by a speedy repentance, as she saw Mr. Berkeley's eyes fixed upon her. Mrs. Walter's warning flashed unpleasantly across her mind.

I do not agree with my sisters, Martha and Jane, that men are more inconstant than women. It is merely that they have more to occupy their minds. They are not so much inconstant as forgetful. For instance, Mr. Berkeley left Digby Manor to mix again in pleasant society, amongst people who knew nothing of the Croftons, and could not name them to him, but Lucy Crofton went home to the ordinary quiet routine of her life, with a good deal to keep up her recollection of the last amusing days spent in his society.

Walter quoted Mr. Berkeley; Mrs. Walter

constantly alluded to .Digby Manor; and when Lucy went to see Miss Walcott she too was full of interest about the whole party, for Mrs. Digby had filled her carriage with the guests at the Manor House and taken them to pay a round of country visits, and Miss Walcott had not been beneath the notice of the great lady of the neighbourhood.

"What did you think of Mrs. Digby?" asked Lucy, when she was seated in her usual chair opposite the white cap, the black wig, and the piercing black eyes of the little lady at Woodbine Cottage.

"Mrs. Digby! Nonsense child!" said Miss Walcott, with a little angry bleat. "Who thinks of Mrs. Digby? There's nothing to say or to think. You might as well talk of the inside of a looking-glass."

"Well, then," said Lucy, laughing, "tell me whether you do not think Miss Spencer beautiful."

"Hum!" said Miss Walcott, not at first attending to Lucy's question, whilst her bright eyes were looking sharply through her. "You look well. I suppose some one talked to you, and made you talk. It does young people good." And then answering Lucy's question, now that she had made her own comments, she said, "I neither know nor care whether Miss Spencer is beautiful! She's better! she's up to fun. Why, bless you, my dear, we chuckled together as if we'd seen into one another's thoughts. She did not mind my cap, nor my wig! not she! You may call her eyes beautiful if you will. They are windows to her soul, just as eyes are meant to be; not bits of stained glass to prevent your seeing out or in. What's the tall man's name? Berkeley?" she repeated, as Lucy answered. "You don't always speak loud enough, my dear; you must try to cure yourself of that habit. Berkeley, did you say?"

"Yes," said Lucy, blushing, she did not know why. What would Miss Walcott say of him? But Miss Walcott was silent. "How very tiresome!" Lucy thought. She wanted her opinion.

Presently, Miss Walcott gave her little short, bleating laugh, telling of great inward amusement. "I could listen to him for an hour without speaking a word," she said at length. "Berkeley, did you say, my dear?"

"Yes," said Lucy, but she was not displeased this time.

"Yes; I could listen to him for an hour without saying a word. Mr. Berkeley is a pleasant, clever man. I hope he will come again."

CHAPTER V.

As nothing more was heard of the recluse at Hulse House, Mrs. Walter Crofton was more fully convinced than ever that he had taken the place on purpose to annoy her. If he meant to shut himself up, why did he come there? It was not at all the house for a man to shut himself up in. It was very rude to the neighbourhood, and especially to Mr. Crofton; she thought it ought to be resented.

"How, my dear?" was Walter's question.

"How, Mr. Crofton," said Mrs. Walter, rather puzzled. "How? Why I certainly should not speak to him if I saw him. No one in the parish ought to be allowed to speak to him."

"But that is just what he wishes," said Walter.

"Now, Mr. Crofton, how can you be so provoking, when you know exactly what I mean; but I can only repeat again what I have said a hundred times already, that it is a positive crime to have let such a man take Hulse House."

Whilst Mrs. Crofton stormed out her angry invectives against the recluse, Lucy thought of him with a very different feeling. She pitied him, and wished that her brother Walter could gain admission to that desolate house. If there was not insanity, there must be sorrow there. I often wonder with what power the kind wishes of his neighbours was resisted, and imagine how Lucy looked at the chimneys of the old gray house whenever they drove along the village road, and how she sighed for its sad inhabitant, and wondered what his thoughts could be. Her own were divided from him just now by a very agreeable interlude, for at the end of a few weeks Miss Spencer was again at Digby Manor, and Lucy was invited to meet her.

As Mrs. Walter wanted some one to talk to when Lucy was gone, she comforted herself by going to Woodbine Cottage.

"Lucy is gone again," she said, rather bitterly, to the little lady; "and I am left at home, with all the cares of housekeeping upon me, and no one to speak to all the morning, for, as you know, Walter is out from breakfast till dinner time, on his parish rounds."

"A very good thing too!" broke in Miss Walcott; "a man poking about a house all morning is intolerable; they chill the room or they heat it; their long legs are always in the way. They take the best arm-chair, and rumple the chintz with their fidgetty ways. Thank God, I never married! but you can't help yourself now, Mrs. Walter. You've got a husband, and it's a blessing he is busy all the morning in the parish."

"Not at all!" chimed in Mrs. Walter; "I always give Walter a good stout morocco leather chair."

"Morocco leather chair!" darted in Miss Walcott; "why then, there he sits, creaking and sliding, and making such a din and clatter in your ears! Morocco leather! I would put my husband in a deep eider down pillowed chair, and let him go into a quiet doze. Leather! slipping and creaking! I've no doubt Mr. Colville sits in a morocco leather chair!"

"Mr. Colville!" exclaimed Mrs. Walter. "You don't mean that any one has seen Mr. Colville sitting in his arm-chair?"

Mrs. Walter generally talked so fast that she scarcely attended to Miss Walcott's running fire of comments; and so they often went on almost at cross purposes.

"Seen him!" she said. "Why should any one care to see a man that locks himself in as if the world were too big for him? Who cares to go and poke their nose down into a dark, damp hole, to look at a frog, because it has taken a whim to jump into it?"

"Oh! Hulse House is not at all damp or dark!" cut in Mrs. Walter; "and I never heard of the frogs getting into the cellars."

Miss Walcott was not to be stopped—"And you never heard of cobwebs to catch flies, I suppose?"

"Oh," said Mrs. Walter, "though Mr. Colville is a recluse, I know he has an excellent housemaid."

"I wish he had a dozen!" chimed in Miss Walcott, "for they would soon drive him out of the house."

"Indeed, that's just what I wish!" said Mrs. Walter; "and I tell Walter so over and over again. If he could but be driven out of the house, we might get a pleasant, sociable neighbour. It would be such an advantage for poor Lucy."

CHAPTER VI.

It is a fine evening in the month of August, some days after Mrs. Crofton's visit to Woodbine Cottage. Little Miss Walcott sits in her cheerful room, looking out at the long line of road leading from Hulse Village. She has been reading; she is placid; she loves to see the broad patches of light and shade, as the evening closes in, and she likes to see the cottage children playing on the wide, grassy margin of the road.

In the street-like village there are some pretty, old-fashioned cottages, with gay gardens before them; the whitewashed porches are covered with roses and honeysuckles; there are little groups of people scattered about here and there; two or three young girls chatting and laughing gaily; some sunburnt boys, full of glee at a game of football; some elderly women coming home, and stopping to have a neighbourly gossip with each other;

four or five men with workmen's dress, discussing parish affairs, and parting with a hearty "goodnight." There is a look of life, of cheerfulness, and of prosperity, about the place—genuine mirth amongst the children, more quiet fun amongst the elders.

At a little distance from the busiest part of the village is a handsome stone wall, skirting the road. On one side of this wall is all this life, gaiety, and activity; on the other, slowly riding along, is a solitary horseman. He hears the distant sounds of mirth—nay, he even hears the words of friendly talk of some of the labourers as they trudge along the road after their day's work; he hears the song of the farmers' servant girls as they pass by with their milk pails; the schoolboy's eager consultation with his compeers about some fishing frolic for the early morning; a mother's proud "Come along Polly—trot on Jack, there's my brave little man," as she walks briskly home with her little ones from a neighbouring farmhouse.

There is sunshine and energy outside that high, dull wall. The road along which the horseman so slowly rides is already in shade—the tall trees, which conceal the wall, cast their long shadows upon it. The rider felt a chill—he slightly shivered—he had just descended from a high and open piece of ground into the shade. He looked up to see the reason for the chill—the handsome stone wall and stately trees were the barrier between himself and the sunshine, and the stir of life without. He smiled bitterly.

"Yes," he thought, "I am cut off from the business and the cheerfulness of life;" and his face became dark with half-angry despondence. The children's chirruping voices were again heard outside.

"Good granny—I love granny!" sung out one little voice.

"And uncle, too," said the hearty mother. "Dost not love Uncle Jem?"

"Polly love Uncle Jem!" said another lisping voice.

"Oh, oh!" laughed the proud mother; "what, he carried my Polly, did he?—good Uncle Jem!" and the voices from the sunny side of the wall passed away.

Arthur Colville proceeded in the shade, and the trees thickened round him, but there was no gloom in those broad, deep shadows, to equal the gloom of his own mind.

When we are old, it is difficult to remember the

hopefulness of youth. I would not try to destroy this cheerful, animating delusion in any young person; depend upon it, it was not put into our natures for nothing. I love my little heroine all the better because she is indulging in delightful visions of faultless friends, of progressive self-improvement, of resuscitated recluses, sobered drunkards, well-fed donkies, and mended roads, as she drives along under the high wall of Hulse House, and is almost overturned by a drunken man's donkey-cart drawn by a very lean donkey, and is half shaken to pieces in going over a very rough bit of road, which is leading her in due course of time to Digby Manor.

The Digbys gave her a warm welcome this time. Mr. Digby told her a story about an enamel snuff-box of his great grandfather's. Mrs. Digby looked at her admiringly, and seemed to regard her as Miss Spencer's pretty new plaything. But Agnes herself thought fit to saunter away into the flower-garden as soon as she had seen Lucy safely landed.

Agnes wandered on as if tempted by the beauty of the afternoon, but in truth she did not notice it; her mind was with the past instead of the present. She walked now with quick and hurried steps; then with lingering ones, as if influenced by her thoughts—sometimes trying to drive them away, sometimes fondly detaining them—until her reverie was broken into by the sound of a shrill whistle.

She looked up, and at the turn of the walk she saw a young man hurrying along in full cry after a truant dog, which was rustling and snuffling about in the bushes edging the walk. Miss Spencer started, and then, as she saw the face and figure of the knight of the whistle, she felt a strong inclination to laugh, from the very great contrast which they bore to something she had been dwelling upon in her own mind. This inclination was not resisted. She stood watching the approach of the hero, with the sunny smiles playing round her mouth, and at length she actually indulged in a hearty fit of laughter, whilst Barker Preston, for he it was, came up, and stood looking rather bewildered at first, but at length smiling, and at last joining heartily in the laugh.

"Upon my word, Miss Spencer, but I don't understand this," he said at length. "It is a capital joke, I am sure," and he laughed again, as Agnes's merriment continued, "but for the life of me I can't make out what it is."

When Agnes could speak, she said, "I beg you ten thousand pardons, Mr. Preston. Don't ask me what I was laughing at, for I really don't know myself: only it was you—you, I am certain! Be flattered, be happy and grateful, Mr. Preston, that you have given me any amusement!"

"And, indeed, I am very happy, Miss Spencer," said Mr. Preston; "though you really should not make too much of a joke of me."

"Oh, never mind," said Agnes, "I was not making any joke of you. I laughed in sober sadness, I can assure you. And now let us walk back to the house together. There is your dog returned—a beautiful dog! What is its name?"

"Rover," said Barker Preston.

"An appropriate name," said Agnes.

"I am glad you admire him," continued Barker Preston. "He is a capital dog," patting him, and looking fondly at him; and Agnes had done exactly what she intended—flattered Mr. Preston in his most vulnerable point. To be sure, he was too thoroughly good-humoured to take offence, but Agnes could not be certain of this. She caressed the dog, but when her admiration was bringing on her the faithful account of its pedigree, and all its good qualities, she quickened her steps, and bid it gallop away and show itself in the distance, and before Barker Preston could begin the subject again, she had slided into another.

"So you have got a wild man of the woods caged in a large cage somewhere about here," she said. "Have you ever peeped through the bars, Mr. Preston?"

"No, no!" laughed Mr. Preston; "I can't manage that."

"Not managed to take a peep!" exclaimed Agnes; "what want of enterprise! I am wild to see him, and I will do so, let bars or bolts interfere as they may! But first I must hear about him. Is he young or old?"

"Old!" said Preston. "No, indeed!—a fine, tall, handsome young man, and as rich as Crœsus; and, it's a strange story! do you know it Miss Spencer?"

Agnes shook her head and smiled, but it was evident she was impatient; she never could endure being bored. Her look said *get on!* and Barker Preston did "get on."

"Well, then, I'll tell you. It's said it's all for grief."

"What is all for grief?" exclaimed Agnes.

"Oh! Miss Spencer, you are so quick upon me," said Preston, laughing. "I meant the shutting up was all for grief; and he has made a vow, I'm told, never to speak to any one again."

"That was a silly vow," said Agnes, gaily, and

the next instant she uttered a slight scream. " Oh, my hand, my hand!" she cried out, standing still as if in pain.

" Bless me, what is the matter?" said Barker Preston, very much alarmed, looking first at Miss Spencer's face and then at her delicate little hand.

" What is the matter?" said Agnes, again half laughing. " My hand is the matter; it gives me such pain—such pain!"

Mr. Preston looked very sorry. " What is to be done for it?" he said, anxiously.

" Nothing at all," said Agnes, " for it is quite well again, thank you. Don't you know that sort of pain sometimes passes off in a minute?" looking up at him and smiling as she walked briskly on.

" Certainly, it was very soon over," said Preston, "and I am very glad of it; but, as I was saying......"

" Oh, pray don't go back to an old subject! It will certainly bring back the pain. Let us have something new; and, by the by, I think you know the Croftons? Miss Crofton came here a few minutes ago."

" Indeed," said Mr. Preston, eagerly, and he quickened his steps.

" She is a very delightful person," said Agnes.

"Ah, yes," was Preston's hesitating reply, looking after his dog.

"I don't know any one I feel so much inclined to love," Agnes added.

"And that is exactly what I feel!" said Barker Preston enthusiastically, completely thrown off his guard by Agnes's praise of Lucy.

CHAPTER VII.

THAT evening at Digby Manor was rather a dull one; Miss Spencer had a headache, and would not or could not talk; Mr. Godfrey was there, as usual, and as indolent as ever.

The happiest person in the room was Barker Preston. Whenever Lucy was not occupied in attending to Mr. Spencer, who had seated himself by her, he was able to talk to her; or, as he would have expressed it, to have a full cry every now and then, a capital chase, and in at the death. When Lucy turned to Mr. Spencer, he consoled himself by watching her countenance. As he would have said, "It was good sport watching the ins and outs. Nothing like it for letting the cat out of the bag. A smile was a view holloa to the thoughts. Then away you go—thundering along, open ground all the way, till you get to a dead halt with a grave look; that tells you to beware

—private property, and the gate locked: so, taking a peep inside, you stand patiently waiting till you catch him again on the other side in a curl of the lip, or a faint blush, and then off—tally-ho! again. You see his tricks through and through—that is, you see to Miss Crofton's heart, and you can't see any harm there—not a deep ditch or an awkward fence all through it."

On the following day, as if to make up for her dulness on the preceding evening, Agnes Spencer was unusually gay. She chose to amuse herself by making Barker Preston tell hunting anecdotes and describe a chase. Mr. Godfrey listened in amazement, and wished very much that Miss Spencer would have sat down within talking distance of him. He could not make the effort of following her about; for really she was first in the library, then the saloon, then the drawing-room, then dancing about the garden like a sylph or a spirit of air.

As the day was fine, Agnes proposed a drive in the pony-carriage for herself and Lucy.

"Mr. Preston, you may ride with us, if you like," she said gaily, turning to him; "supposing you keep yourself either as a part of the background or as a striking object in the distance. But you must not interrupt my conversation with Miss Crofton unless it happens to flag."

No other person could have said this without giving offence, but there was something flattering in the playfulness of Miss Spencer's impertinence. Barker Preston laughed, and said he would do his best to keep out of the way, if she would only allow him to ride the same road.

"Then, Mrs. Digby," said she, "may I order the pony-carriage?" ringing the bell at the same time; and the carriage was ordered. Lucy was amused and surprised, but Mrs. Digby only whispered to Mr. Godfrey, "What a dear, engaging creature she is!" and was quite delighted to take Miss Spencer's orders, and Agnes was aware that she was whenever she took the trouble to think about it; but her orders were usually given to suit her own convenience, and if the Digbys' house, or horses, or servants could be useful in gratifying a whim she made use of them with a saucy independence that put a stop to a "nay." Lucy thought her wrong; she thought it would have been better to check the whim, and Agnes thought so herself. As they drove along that day she said to Lucy—

"I have the misfortune to be a spoilt child, and there is no one so pitiable. We eat up our cake, and want it when it is gone, and don't enjoy it when we have it. And the worst of it is, that a contradiction comes very sharply when we are unused to it—too sharply for us to profit by it! it overwhelms instead of softening. Do you see that dark cloud hanging over the hill? what a pity it seems that it should darken that beautiful blue sky; but it has been too bright inthe early morning, and the cloud will soon spread over the whole. It will then strike us less, but it will be more gloomy!"

There was a curious mixture of jest and earnest in her manner, as she gazed up into the sky, and seemed to be reading a history of her own life and feelings in the grandly sailing clouds, which were every moment obscuring more and more of the heavens.

"I can see in all this a likeness to my own life," she said. "The morning was quite unclouded; it was far too prosperous. It must have been evident to any one but myself that clouds and storms would come; but I never dreamt of it! I was happy, and gay, and thoughtless! But the cloud came for all that. It came and spread, just as you see that huge cloud spreading over us now. It spread, and it will spread, till everything becomes involved in its gloom."

Miss Spencer's voice had grown sad, and even faltering, as she uttered the last words, but Lucy had hardly time to imagine it before she was roused and surprised by a lively exclamation—

"Look, Miss Crofton!" Agnes said, gaily; "look at our gallant knight! 'He loves and he rides away.' Let us overtake him!" and she set the ponies off at a brisk pace, and Mr. Preston pulled in his horse and was soon, by Agnes Spencer's desire, riding at the side of the carriage. A few drops of rain began to fall.

"What will become of us!" said Agnes, in a voice of alarm. "We shall be wet through! Mr. Preston is there no house near where we can take shelter?"

"There is one house," said Mr. Preston, "if you could get into it, and that is Hulse; but you could not get into it, I fear, if it was raining cats and dogs."

"Hulse! are we really close to Hulse?" said Agnes, with eagerness that almost seemed like affection; "then I am determined I will get shelter there. Which is the road to it, Mr. Preston? Show me the road, and I will drive in directly, and let Mr. What's-his-name refuse admittance if he can!"

Barker Preston pointed out the way, but said, "It's of no use, for it is many miles off, and there is the lodge first—though, to be sure, you might perhaps shelter there."

Agnes had not waited to hear the end of his speech. She was driving quickly along the road to the lodge, not attending to Lucy's quiet expostulation, except by saying, "Never mind! we shall see when we get there! I am determined to try!"

They reached the lodge; no one came to the gate; it was locked. The door of the lodge was inside. Agnes uttered an impatient exclamation, and looked really annoyed, much more so than Lucy thought reasonable on such a small occasion, for the rain had ceased.

"Call, Mr. Preston! Shake the gate, or knock!" she said, impatiently.

Barker Preston knocked and called, but no one came. "We must turn back, I fear; and indeed the rain is gone," he said; "I don't feel it at all."

"I shall not turn till I have seen some one here," said Agnes, decidedly. "Look, Mr. Preston, there is a cottage not far off; suppose you go there and ask where the gatekeeper is."

Barker Preston demurred; he thought Miss Spencer a little foolish, but she repeated her wish so decidedly and earnestly that he could not refuse. He was too good-natured ever to withstand much solicitation; so he galloped off.

"I fear we shall not get in," Lucy said.

"Oh! yes we shall," said Agnes, rather pettishly. Her temper seemed to fail under the disappointment of her whim; but then, as if recollecting herself, she turned to Lucy and laughed at her own folly. "I told you I was a spoilt child," she said. "But what can keep Mr. Preston so long?" she added, again impatiently.

"Ah! there he is!" she said, as at length he appeared galloping towards them.

"She is coming!" he exclaimed, as he rode up; "the old woman is coming, Miss Spencer, and then you can hold a parley; but the people up there say you may as well attempt to fly, as to get within those gates."

"Then I will attempt to fly," said Agnes, with rather playful perverseness in her tone. "But we shall wait for ever for this old woman; you should have brought her on your horse, Mr. Preston. Oh, there she comes!" and the old woman came to the gate. "Will you open the gate for us, if you please?" said Agnes, with her most winning smile.

Mr. Preston watched her with great interest, it was so amusing to see the determined flattery of her manner.

The old woman was so much struck with the beautiful smile and sweet voice of the lady that it went much against her feelings to refuse, but she did so. She shook her head. "I am very sorry to say I can't, ma'am."

"Can't!" said Agnes, affecting surprise; "oh! you are mistaken; though some persons are refused admittance, I think you will remember that you had no order to send us away."

"Every one was to be sent back," said the woman; "those were my orders. Mr. Hodson told me himself."

"And who is Mr. Hodson?" said Agnes, still speaking in her softest voice.

"He is the head man—the vally, or butler, or something of that sort, I believe," said the old woman.

"Oh, yes! but you did not see Mr. Colville himself?" said Agnes.

"No, he did not speak to me; he seldom does to never a one! and he has only rode this way once since he comed amongst us."

"And how did he look?" said Agnes, eagerly.

"Perhaps you know him, ma'am?" said the woman, in her turn looking inquisitive.

Agnes did not answer quickly; "Mr. Colville has friends, you know, as we all have," was her reply; and then she said, *sotto voce*, to Lucy, "If I say I do'nt know him, we shall never get admitted. How did he look when you saw him?" she said to the woman, repeating her question.

"I could not see him very plain, but he looked sadly, I thought, poor gentleman; but he'd a very pleasant smile when he spoke to my John, who was making the ditch there, and John—that's my husband—said, says he, 'He was quite the gentleman, but spoke low and fainty like, as if he was sad at heart.' He was a fine tall figure of a man, only he stooped a little."

"And he was pale?" said Agnes, who had been listening intently, with her usual whimsicality of interest.

"Yes, ma'am; very pale!"

"And does he ride much?"

"Yes, I believe so, but he seldom quits the grounds, excepting it is late in the evening; but he generally goes through the other lodge. I fear he is in very poor health and spirits, and that makes him not like to see any company."

"You don't mean that his mind is affected?" said Agnes, scornfully.

"Oh, dear, bless me, no, ma'am! He is quite rational like, only down in his spirits."

"Is he kind to you?" said Agnes, more quietly, as if getting rather bored with the subject.

"Oh, yes, ma'am! he is very open handed; but I always think as he gets out of the way, if he can."

Agnes had perhaps forgotten her wish to enter the lodge gates, whilst she stayed quietly talking to the old woman. At length, however, she said, "And now will you, if you please, unlock the gate, for I can wait no longer?"

The old woman looked wistfully at the gate, then at Agnes, but she shook her head. "Indeed, ma'am, I can't! I can't, indeed! I wish I could!"

"Well, perhaps when next I come you will have fresh orders," said Agnes; and giving her some money, she turned the carriage round, and they were soon quickly proceeding back again on the road to the Manor House, as if forgetting that any one was in the carriage with her, and depended on her whims.

"It is a pretty-looking place," she remarked at length, to Lucy. And then, instead of saying more on the subject which had seemed for the time to interest her even to folly, with her usual fickleness she turned to another, and said not a word more about Hulse and Mr. Colville.

The first words Lucy heard from Miss Spencer, as she followed her into the drawing-room at Digby Manor, were, "Ah, Mr. Berkeley! what brought you here? How glad I am to see you!" and Lucy walked in, not to repeat the words,

but, I am afraid, to echo them in her heart.
There was a bright sparkle in her eyes, and a
pretty colour on her cheeks, as she saw him, and
there was also a smile on his face, as he looked at
her, and shook hands, that seemed to answer
Miss Spencer's question, of "What brought you
here?"

"Perhaps," said my sister Jane, with a gentle
sigh, as I read this last sentence, "perhaps he is
not so very satirical after all!" But Martha
slightly frowned at her, and bid her not to interrupt me with nonsensical comments. "The characters were not yet unfolded," she said; and with
this observation I proceeded to my next remark,
that,

Barker Preston thought Lucy looked more than
usually pretty that evening, as Mr. Berkeley sat
beside her. "She used to have nothing to do but
to smile at me when we were together at the
Parsonage!" he thought, "but she never looked
quite so happy as she does now. Her work does
not get on so quickly, either!" he thought. "Her
fingers used to move as steadily as a good hack
along the road, but now it's all by fits and starts—
and look!—now is that blush because she has made

a wrong stitch, or because—but never mind!" he mused on, "I like to see her happy!" and with this good-natured conclusion, worthy of a grand flourish of trumpets, had he only been a hero, Barker Preston's soliloquy ended.

Mrs. Digby asked him to play *écarte* with her; and he had no inclination to refuse.

"Miss Spencer is remarkably industrious this evening," he remarked, as he looked at Agnes, who was winding silks, whilst Mr. Godfrey held the skeins for her.

"She is always enthusiastic, you know," said Mrs. Digby, "in whatever she undertakes. It is your deal, Mr. Preston."

There had been a little malicious pleasure this evening in Miss Spencer's enthusiasm for silk-winding. It was an amusement invented at the moment, to force Mr. Godfrey into exertion. She took care that he could not possibly lean back in his chair, or even on the side of it, whilst he held the silk. She detained him in an upright position, got the silk a little entangled every now and then, and once or twice allowed the winder to slip out of her hands on to the floor.

"Will you be so kind as to pick it up?" was her careless command, as she sat indolently waiting for him to conquer the difficulty of moving his legs and arms. A very bright smile was the reward, as he presented the silk, and though very much fatigued, he was so much flattered and entertained by her amusing conversation that he could not release himself.

"You ran away and left us this morning," he said; "it was terribly dull without you."

"Why, then, did not you come with us?" said Agnes.

"Why, what could I do?" said he, shrugging his shoulders, and raising his eyebrows with a look of self-commiseration. "Nothing is so tiring as a drive with nothing to see."

"Certainly it is very bad," said Agnes. "However, I saw a great deal to-day."

"Did you?" said Mr. Godfrey, looking rather surprised.

"Oh, Mr. Godfrey, you are letting it fall!" she exclaimed, in a voice of despair. "I believe you must be so good as to hold the silk a little more this way. When your arm rests the very least in the world on the table, the silk always gets twisted."

"I beg your pardon," said Mr. Godfrey, penitently. "Do you always wind your own silks?" he added, doubtingly.

"Oh no, very seldom. It was a sudden whim,

and, as you are so kind as to hold the skeins, I hope to finish this large set whilst I am here." She stooped down, pretending to undo a knot, but in reality to conceal the smile which was playing about the corners of her mouth.

"Well, I will release you for to-day," she exclaimed, at length, tired of entertaining herself at his expense. "A thousand thanks. Mrs. Digby, you will not ask me to sing, so I am going to ask myself."

"I am delighted!" said Mrs. Digby; and Agnes sat down to the instrument and George Berkeley deserted Lucy to go and listen to her.

CHAPTER VIII.

THE next day it did nothing but rain—drives, walks, rides, all at an end. Mr. Digby wondered it should rain, as he had intended taking the party to see Helmsworth.

"I had made the plan two days ago," he said. "I had arranged it completely, and even taken the trouble to order a new open carriage to be ready a week sooner than I at first intended. It is very odd that it should rain! I am really annoyed! I am surprised! Mr. Preston will you have the goodness to feel out at that window whether it still rains?"

Mr. Preston returned with an account that it rained faster than ever.

"Indeed!" said Mr. Digby, "and my arrangements were quite perfect. Still raining! Really! I had no idea of this!"

"A good moral lesson," said Agnes, in a low voice to Mr. Berkeley, who looked grave.

"We must alter the well known adage for Mr. Digby," he said. "'*L'homme arrange et Dieu derange*' would be more appropriate than the old, humble saying, '*L'homme propose et Dieu dispose.*'"

If Mr. Digby was too callous or frivolous to care for the rebuke, Lucy honoured George Berkeley for it, and almost unconsciously her eyes rested on his face with a glowing look of approval. I think George Berkeley saw it; for when Lucy turned away he watched her for some time—half inquisitively.

"Suppose we have a grand musical practice, Miss Crofton," said Agnes, when they adjourned to the drawing-room. "We will play all our duets twice over, repeating every part, and then we will sing all our songs, stopping at every wrong note. Mr. Berkeley, you may come and help us in going wrong, and Mr. Preston, you may *encore* us when we go right. In this way we shall get through the morning pretty well, I think."

"Get through the morning!" exclaimed George Berkeley; "as if there were any difficulty! As for me, the difficulty is how to keep it long enough," and he glanced at Lucy.

The hours, in truth, did not hang heavily on

that day at Digby Manor; Agnes Spencer's spirits seemed to rise as the rain fell. There was a good deal of music, but there was something besides music to make the hours pass pleasantly. Agnes, Lucy, and Mr. Berkeley had many talks together—grave, gay, foolish, and wise. I am old now, and these pleasant, eager conversations do not belong to my years. We old people talk on useful, practical subjects, or we prose of the past, or we relate anecdotes; but the sort of talk I mean—the sort which passed that day between those three—belongs essentially to youth; it was the broaching of new ideas, and making discoveries of each other's opinions and sentiments. I well remember talks such as these! They can never be again, but what a charm there was about them! Yes, my dear little heroine, no wonder your eyes have such a deep, earnest, happy look, as you slowly glide along the large hall, and go to your own room, to think it all over before dressing time! She, and Miss Spencer, and Mr. Berkeley, had become more than mere acquaintance since the morning.

But it is curious how quickly our sentiments may change in society! On the very evening of that friendly morning, Lucy accidentally heard Mrs. Digby reproach Mr. Berkeley for his long absence from the neighbourhood, and she heard him very civilly regret that " circumstances " had prevented him from coming sooner.

" What circumstances ?" she thought, and there rushed upon her mind visions of magnificent country houses, delightful hosts and hostesses—sons and daughters who were fitting companions to George Berkeley—society where other George Berkeleys were to be found—everything, in short, superior to herself, and Mrs. Walter, and the parsonage.

Mr. Berkeley was not by her at dinner, and in the early part of the evening he was much engaged in talking with others. The *circumstances* that kept him out of the neighbourhood of the parsonage became more vivid and depressing. Out of the hundred lovely young ladies he might have met, one was singled out, supreme in beauty. There she sat in her queen-like superiority, Mr. Berkeley at her side, speaking to her in a low earnest voice—looking at her with an anxious, expressive look. Lucy could bear it no longer! It made her unhappy! She must rouse herself! It could be nothing but a vile, unamiable fit of envy. She determined to shake it off. She bravely raised her head; and then, strange to say, Mr. Berkeley's eyes met her's—the low and tender tones of his voice greeted her ears—he was soon seated by her, and one and all of these delightful people he was constantly in the habit of meeting were forgotten by her, if they were but too well remembered by him.

How long Lucy Crofton might have thought of him that night, after she retired to her room, I cannot say, for her mind was diverted into a new channel. Miss Spencer came in; she sat down; she looked pale and harassed.

"It is a wearisome world, after all," said she, and then she was silent.

"Do you think so?" was Lucy's quick reply.

"Yes, I do!" said Agnes, whilst a smile flashed across her face, amused for a moment by the evident contrast in their feelings. But the smile soon passed. "Yes I do!" she said; "who can help it, when every day is full of annoyances and Mrs. Digbys. I have been worn to death! Wearied, harassed, irritated! Oh, Miss Crofton!" she added, in a voice of emotion, "you do not know what it is to have one bitter subject of remembrance clinging to you, which some fool unconsciously or spitefully grates, and rubs, and hangs upon, till you shrink and writhe under it! She has been torturing me! I tried to laugh! I tried to make a jest of it! I am sure my father heard my laugh; he turned so quickly round to look at me. It must have been a horribly discordant sound, if it jarred on the ear as it did on my heart; but that odious woman could not perceive it, or she perceived it and liked it. She went on till every nerve seemed touched and tingling! I believe we have all of us a history," she added, after a pause, "or perhaps there are some quiet natures who dose through life without any stirring, moving incidents. There is pain in the other line, and yet I would not be without it," she added, with half a smile. " The stir and tumult of emotion have a pleasure in them, even if pain must accompany or follow in their wake. I would not be the dull last leaf, hanging on the sleeping branch. No! I would have been the vigorous, dancing leaf that was whirled away the soonest, because it had lived its little life with vigour and animation."

Lucy felt with Agnes, but she thought that the sentiment was carried to the extreme; there was a wide interval in her mind between the dosing and the whirling existence.

Agnes continued—" Whether I would or no, there have been sharp pains and lively pleasures in my life as yet. Here is a little ring that shall talk for me," she said, with her curious mixture of playfulness and gravity, as she pointed to a ring on the third finger of her left hand. "Dear little ring! hated, yet loved!"

Lucy saw that the eyes of Agnes were moist with tears as she spoke half musingly, and looked at the ring.

"Yes," she said, "this little ring is a history in itself! It was placed here by some one, no matter whom! It was left here by some one, no matter for how long! but it got a home and a friendship here. It is said that a little vessel flows direct from the heart to this magical finger. It may be so! for the ring that encircled the finger twined round the heart too, and then it was suddenly taken away by some one—I can't say who!—two had a share in it, but perhaps the blame rested with one; but the pain fell hard on one and perhaps on both!"

She paused; her mind seemed far away in the past; but then she continued—"And yet the ring came back! but it was no longer the same. It brought a sting with it, and sometimes a careless hand presses it, and the sting runs in and reaches by that same tie of blood to the heart."

She stopped. Lucy saw that tears were rolling down her cheeks, but she wiped them away. Lucy's expression seemed to soothe her.

"When I first saw you I knew that you would understand me," she said, gently. " I knew that I could talk to you without having to explain my meaning ; and that if I happened to be sad you would not tell me to be merry. I believe you to be true and safe, and it does me good to be with you. But I am afraid of you," she added, in her own odd, whimsical way.

" Afraid of me !" said Lucy, with a look of wondering incredulity.

" Yes ;" Agnes continued, " because you have not a wrong or a wicked thought in your head or your heart, and I have a crowd of them."

Lucy almost unconsciously gave a little start.

" Yes, there it is," said Agnes, half laughing. " Now I am afraid of you ! It is one of your grave, *surprised* looks that I fear."

" I will try not to look surprised or grave again," said Lucy.

" And then you would not be Lucy Crofton, and I should not love you ! No, be yourself, and show me by your looks when I am wrong. Ah ! if I had always had those looks to guard me !" and she spoke with sad, almost with bitter feeling.

The next day was all sunshine; every tree came out of the wash beautifully got up, as the washerwomen would say; every blade of grass

E 5

seemed starched and stiffened; all clean, spruce, and uncrumpled. There had been a very slight frostiness in the air at night, and the sun rose without a breath of wind, and shone steadily and brightly all day. It was a beautiful day for a drive, and at breakfast Mr. Digby expressed his approval, and the excursion to Helmsworth took place. Every one knows what it is, or guesses what it might be to spend a long day amongst beautiful scenery, in perfectly delicious weather, with exactly the people whom you consider the pleasantest in the world.

This was the case with Lucy Crofton, and I shall not weaken the pretty, glowing picture which any reader's imagination may call up, by trying to describe it according to the more sober colouring of my own fancy.

"Are you tired?" Mr. Berkeley said, as he handed Lucy from the carriage when they returned in the evening to Digby Manor.

"Tired!" said Lucy, and her face looked so bright and pretty, that it was excusable in George Berkeley slightly to press her hand as he helped her to alight.

"Tired!" echoed Agnes Spencer. "Who dares speak of being tired? It has been a day of days!"

CHAPTER IX.

Lucy's younger brother, Edward, came to Digby Manor the next day. Miss Spencer was full of anxiety to see him. Agnes had not asked Lucy any questions about him, for she wished to get her own impression fresh and unbiassed. She was certain of one thing, and that was that Lucy loved this brother Edward with peculiar affection, and Agnes had no fear, therefore, of letting her fancy run wild in adorning him with every charm. Her face was in a glow of animation as he came in, and it was almost ludicrous to see the change on her countenance as she watched his introduction to the Digbys. Edward Crofton was not plain; he had good features, and a tall, well-made figure; but he was a dull-looking young man, and he spoke in a quiet, monotonous voice; and as he sat there so indolently passive, the enthusiasm and the indignation of Agnes were struggling which should cool down the fastest. He was evidently a dull, prosy person, with a manner and character of sleepy, immoveable quiet. Agnes was extremely vexed. She was determined not to talk to him more than necessary, and she only said a few words from a sense of duty as she sat by him at dinner. But as she spoke, a droll, comic look in his face surprised her. She turned quickly round to examine it. But the face had resumed its sleepy expression, and she returned to her first vexing belief, that Lucy's brother was dull! It was too provoking! She certainly would not waste any more words upon him!

But this resolution was strangely frustrated by Edward Crofton himself. He began to talk, rather, as it seemed, because he wished to utter his thoughts aloud than as if he cared who or what his neighbour might be. He had not uttered many words in his slow, deliberate way before, to the astonishment of Agnes, she found herself obliged to listen; and before he had rolled on with his flow of ideas through many sentences, Agnes found herself in the height of interest in all that he said; found herself watching with amusement for his little, short, inward laugh, as his deep-set eyes sparkled out of their long, narrow channels, and was finally talking and laughing with him with extreme enjoyment, and owning, too, with great satisfaction, that she had been completely wrong in her first impression of his character. She could scarcely believe, when dinner was over, that the person whose last words she was lingering to hear, and to whom she had so much to say, was the same dull Mr. Crofton by whom she had seated herself in such a fit of disappointed ill-humour at the beginning.

In fact, Edward Crofton was a very clever man; young as he was, he had a more powerful mind, and had perhaps a deeper fund of knowledge than most men of his day. Joined to this, he had a peculiar justness and uprightness of character; he had great simplicity, good-nature, and good temper; he had strong, but not lively affections; he was kind and benevolent, rather than ardently affectionate; he had Walter's utter contempt of humbug and affectation; and there was an under current of drollery which seemed to imbue his whole unexciteable, easy temperament. He had no ambition, unless we may call such the pleasure he had in work, which made him thoroughly master whatever he undertook.

He was but little known as yet, but in after years Edward Crofton was heard of. The breadth and great grasp of his mind worked itself into notice, as it were, in spite of the passive resistance to fame afforded by his own utter contempt for it. Lucy loved to sit and listen to her brother, and to see that odd, droll sparkle come into his eye and the corners of his mouth curl up with some half-malicious bit of fun, when he was assailed by her playful attacks; just as at home he parried Mrs. Walter's less agreeable missiles, with imperturbable good humour.

"I love to get Mr. Edward Crofton on a favourite topic," she heard Miss Spencer say to Mr. Berkeley, "and to hear how his ideas come rolling forth out of that grand, wonderfully comprehensive mind."

Neither did Edward despise Agnes. If she lounged into the library, she slided into such agreeable conversation, that he almost forgot the books, which as yet were his chief idols, and only remembered them when an attempt was made to tear him away from his treasures, by a proposal from Mr. or Mrs. Digby to join in a walking, or riding, or driving party.

And now I must pause. I have introduced the reader to most of those with whom I wish him to be interested, and the last day of Lucy's stay at Digby Manor is come, and Edward Crofton must go again to his office work in London. I cannot exactly say how often his little sister's soft face obtruded itself upon him in the midst of a legal decision, or how many of Miss Spencer's startling ideas flashed across him, to illumine the dingy atmosphere of the office. He was at his work again, and Lucy was once more at the parsonage, and the Spencers and Mr. Berkeley had deserted that lively, luxurious manor house.

"But brother!" broke in my sister Jane, very suddenly. "Was Lucy Crofton little; you always call her your little heroine?"

"Little is a term of endearment," was my answer. "Lucy was little, but not short. Will that satisfy you Jane?"

"How tall?" was the answer, still doubtfully.

"My dear Jane, that is a dangerous question; however, I will tell you. She was about the middle height."

"And her figure?" said the pertinacious Jane.

I shook my head, and then added, "So graceful and slight that every one thought of her as *a dear little thing*; that is all I can tell!"

"That will do," was the answer, with a satisfied nod. "Go on brother;" and I obeyed.

A long tirade from Mrs. Walter on the carelessness of the cook in over-roasting a leg of mutton was Lucy's greeting at home. It did not quite amalgamate with the more *spirituelle* atmosphere from which she had just parted; but a visit to Miss Walcott was more amusing, and as Lucy and Mrs. Walter came to the spruce little garden at Woodbine Cottage, Miss Walcott, from her usual chair, looked out of the window.

"Rose-bud and full-blown rose," was her remark to herself, as she first saw them. "Hum! rose-buds are my fancy, but you must take them as you can, in the bunch! A great, flaunting, full-blown thing, spreading itself over the bud! Pretty little bud! not a thorn about it! Never saw a prettier bud!" she went on muttering to herself as they were coming in.

There was a parley on the stairs between Miss Walcott's maid Sally, and Mrs. Walter, and Miss Walcott went on with a sort of running comment, as the conversation reached her ears.

"Servants! bother! '*Steady under housemaid!*' '*No sweethearts!*' Nonsense! A hearty, healthy, hard-working girl, and no sweetheart! stuff! '*Don't approve of followers,*' nonsense! Sweethearts have had a trick of following after tidy, good-tempered girls since the world began, and they will keep up the habit, Mrs. Walter, let you clatter away as long as you please! Come, Mrs. Walter, come in, come in!" she called out at last, aloud, to Mrs. Walter. "Come in! You need not stand talking on my stairs any longer! We don't know of an under housemaid to suit you, and, Sally, you need not tell Mrs. Crofton you do! All the girls we know have one sweetheart at least, and perhaps a dozen." And in came Mrs. Walter.

"Well, Miss Walcott, whatever you may say, I never will allow my servants to have followers, eating up the bread and cheese, and swilling the beer, in our house."

"Why, then," chimed in Miss Walcott, "tell the girls to choose with discretion, and get lovers that don't like cheese and beer. Here, Lucy, sit down, close to me, child, and you Eliza Crofton, when you have done talking about brooms and dusters, tell me whether you have seen your hermit of Hulse yet?"

"Seen him! No, indeed! and I don't care ever to see such a creature! Here is Lucy, just come from Digby Manor—and there it was! Miss Spencer (you know who I mean), quite a fine lady. Well! she asked to go into Mr. Colville's lodge, to shelter from a violent storm; and what do you think? The old story—the gate locked, and Mr. Colville refused to admit them, even into his lodge, though it was raining torrents."

"Not exactly that," Lucy put in. "All I said was that the lodge gate was locked."

"Yes, yes!" rejoined Mrs. Walter; "you are always making excuses for Mr. Colville! But you owned, I am sure, when I questioned you particularly, that it did rain, and that Miss Spencer drove there for shelter, and could not get in. But it is always the way that my wishes are thwarted! and, in short, the man who let Mr. Colville take Hulse House has much to answer for! Hulse House is a constant annoyance to me! One way or other it is always plaguing me!"

Miss Walcott had given sundry little short, bleating laughs, and uttered various little "hums" and sharp coughs, whilst Mrs. Walter held forth, and she now broke in with, "Should not wonder if Hulse House killed you at last! It will be found at your heart when you die, as sure as Calais was at Queen Mary's."

"I don't care what was at Queen Mary's heart when she died," said Mrs. Walter, angrily; "but I know it is very wearing to mine, to have to be always regretting that large house—that might have had such good tenants in it—just shut up as if it were a prison—and used as I was to plenty of society, without a creature to speak to, excepting just when we go to the Digby's; and even there you see Lucy has been without us!"

"Yes, Lucy shall tell us about it!" said Miss Walcott, "when we have done crying because the moon's not made of green cheese. Come, Lucy, child, tell your sister and me what these people said and did, for we want a little entertainment. We have had the tragedy, now let us have the farce! What did Miss Spencer say and do? Nothing commonplace, I'll be bound for it! She's like the flash of a diamond."

CHAPTER X.

MEANTIME how did the days glide away at Hulse House. We pass through the large hall and enter the library. Arthur Colville sits there reading. A clock on the chimney-piece strikes the hour— it is the self-same hour on which Mr. Berkeley's voice had startled Lucy Crofton out of her reverie at Digby Manor. Mr. Colville started as she had done; but the cause and the effect were as different as possible. No pretty visions of future happiness, no bright enjoyment of the present, danced through his mind. The sound of the clock roused him from his interest in his book. He let his hand fall listlessly over the arm of his chair. In that long, dreary evening, and the many and the many that might follow, what was there to rouse him? There was, in all likelikood, a long life before him—the clock would strike many times, and he might be aroused many times from interest in his book, to the same vague, objectless dejection as now.

He smiled bitterly as he thought "Why did I do it?" and strangely enough another thought intruded. Humanly speaking, the step he had taken excluded all his acquaintance from any knowledge of his conduct; and yet he found himself over and over again shrinking under the fancied sneers or reproofs of his friends, and trying to dignify his selfish, cowardly act into one of grand abandonment of the littlenesses and vices of the outer world.

In the first anguish of bitter disappointment (for he had suffered under a grievous trial) he had flown to solitude as his only refuge from insufferable pain. For a time pride supported him; for, little as he guessed it, he was proud of the pre-eminence of suffering—proud of his fancied courage in bearing self-inflicted solitude.

He strove to dignify the evil he had laid on himself. His watch words of comfort were literary occupation and benevolence to the poor; and he planned improvements and alterations on his new property for the sake of benefitting the oppressed labouring classes, as he would have termed them; for his wounds had come from the higher and not the lower orders.

The cultivation of the mind was his other resource. His library was filled with books, his walls with pictures, and at times he really enjoyed his leisure, for deep reading was a new pleasure to him; but then, again, he looked round the deserted rooms—there was no voice to answer his own—no smile to meet his eyes—his mind had to prey on itself for resources. Vainly did he say, "It is a relief to be alone!" his heart yearned for sympathy; it swelled at times with the vehement desire to be *not* alone.

Solitude was a harbour for sorrow, not a refuge from it; it surrounded and subdued his powers, and if at times he wished to break through his seclusion, his enervated mind made him cling to it with greater bitterness, as he felt his unfitness for the busy life which he had deserted.

It was fortunate for him that he had a safety valve in the necessary intercourse between master and servant. I can hardly speak or write of his servant, William Hodson, without a glow of pride and pleasure. I knew him well; in later times we have often talked together, and I think I now see his honest, open countenance as he speaks to me; touching profitably, with his quiet, calm, good sense, on any subject we happen to discuss. He is a remarkable character, but there are no brilliant qualities to set forth—quiet, staid, and rather reserved—his rare merit was good sense—*common* sense, as has been said, the *most uncommon* of all qualities.

William Hodson had been a page in the household of Colville's father; he had grown up with that reverential attachment to his master's family which was not unusual in our country about half a century back, but which is probably dying away with other remains of feudalism. With strong, self-sacrificing attachment he had secluded himself from the world for his master's sake; his very place of abode was even kept a profound secret from every relation or friend he possessed. Arthur Colville had given Hodson his choice, either to leave or to stay with him; and he insisted on his taking a full week for deliberation. He offered him a handsome annuity and a comfortable home on the old property, if he decided against following his sad fortunes for the future, for Colville was noble in his nature, and he proposed a bribe to induce him to leave, but none to persuade him to stay; and yet no one could half imagine how he clung to the thought of having that one familiar face with him in his misery and loneliness!

After the week's deliberation, on which Mr.

Colville had insisted, when Hodson came to his master's room and said, in his quiet, unmoved manner, "I have made up my mind, sir; I wish to stay with you," Colville's quivering lip, his fervent "thank you," and the hearty grasp he gave the hand of his faithful servant, betrayed what his feelings were.

Mr. Colville's seclusion had dated some years before he entered his last prison house at Hulse, and all Hodson's efforts to arouse his interest in anything beyond himself had as yet been fruitless. He could only watch with pain an unfavourable change in his character—the once eager, light-hearted youth had become a gloomy, irritable man, with whom it was necessary to weigh words and to watch for the right moment to speak.

"But only for a time! only for a time!" he would repeat over and over again to himself. "Better days will come! I must be patient! God bless him, he deserves that I should!"

It is rather agreeable to get away from the gloomy atmosphere of Hulse House to the bustling activity of Mrs. Walter Crofton's ideas, and to the stir of commonplace life in which she is living. She was looking complacently at a delicately perfumed note which she had just opened.

"Another invitation from the Digbys," she exclaimed. "Very civil indeed! Next Thursday—a lucky day! I always like going out on Thursday!"

Lucy knew that Mr. Berkeley was at Digby Manor. She escaped out of doors to talk to the flowers of her pleasure; they had a kind of sympathy in their bloom and freshness; and as her little graceful figure went gliding about on the grass, or her lips were lovingly pressed into the depths of a full-blown rose—she could whisper to them of her joy. Her brother Walter happened to pass by. He was not apt to think much about personal beauty; but there was something irresistibly pleasant in the sight of Lucy at that moment, and he stopped to look at her.

"You are quite a child still, Lucy," he said. "How old are you, really?"

"Seventeen," said Lucy, half ashamed at having to name such an advanced age, as she remembered how little stately her step had been on the grass.

"Ah! that is very old," said Walter with a smile, as he passed on.

CHAPTER XI.

I DON'T know any greater mistake than that of envying a young unmarried man of large fortune, who is much in request in London society. Unless he is happily crossed in love, his whole life is objectless; everything he wishes for is his the moment he asks for it; he has nothing to strive for, he has nothing to do; he has only to amuse himself, and it is trite to a proverb to say that there is no trade so fatiguing.

Healthy youth is full of energy, and activity, and ambitious aspirations, and if there is no wholesome exercise for its exuberance of vigour, it will form to itself less profitable ones, or sink into listless stupor of mind and heart.

I dare say many old men besides myself, and many young ones too, would agree with me in theory; but when they are introduced to the young, rich, unmarried Lord Englefield, who just then honoured Mr. and Mrs. Digby with his presence at Digby Manor, as usual, they sigh and say as they look at him, "I wish our Charley or our Freddy, or our Johnny were as perfectly independent as that lucky fellow, Lord Englefield!" I beg leave to say that if there is any good in Charley, or Freddy, or Johnny, it is probably owing to the fact that they were not as lucky as Lord Englefield, and had they been born to wealth and indolence, I should say to them, "make work for yourselves," for, as old Watts tells us,

"Satan finds some mischief still for idle hands to do;"

and I would din it into their ears and their hearts too, if I could, to work, work, work, if they would save themselves from the most cruel of all fates— either to grow recklessly bad or to live on to become idle, self-indulgent, middle-aged men about town: and as I saw that handsome, well-cared-for youth, Lord Englefield, I shook my head and sighed, on observing the languid, self-satisfied air, which a few years of spoiling had effected on a good, intelligent, active nature.

However, here he is, standing indolently near the window, waiting to be amused, and as the door opens he catches sight of a pretty little figure following the rather showy one of Mrs. Walter Crofton into the drawing-room at Digby Manor, just before dinner time. His eyes light up with a little animation, for here is something new, at any rate.

"Who is she?" he said, in a low voice, to George Berkeley.

There was a half-malicious smile on Mr. Berkeley's face, as he answered, whilst looking at Mrs. Walter Crofton. "Her name is Crofton; I will introduce you, if you like."

"Thank you," was the reply, and off darted Mr. Berkeley, whilst Lord Englefield remained in a pleasurable state of excitement, thinking of the coming introduction. He suddenly found Mr. Berkeley saying to him, "Lord Englefield— Mrs. Crofton. Mrs. Crofton—Lord Englefield," with a sort of speech about the wish for acquaintance, which obliged him to make some civil reply. Mr. Berkeley then wandered back to Lucy, entered into conversation with her, and was ready to offer her his arm when dinner was announced.

"I suppose I ought to be unhappy," he said, when they were seated, "for I have been guilty of a very successful fraud. What do you say to my chances of happiness during dinner?"

"I should say that your punishment is sure to come," said Lucy, laughing.

"And then I will be penitent, and not a moment sooner!" said he. "But I wish you would not promise me unhappiness."

"I did not promise," said Lucy, "I only prophesied, from experience."

"*Your* experience! then I am easy!" he exclaimed, "for you never did an ill-natured thing in your life, I am certain. However," he added, "as the seat next you was my object, it is entirely in your own power to give me the fitting moral lesson!"

Lucy blushed, but did not find any answer ready at the moment.

George Berkeley went on. "It is exactly three weeks and one day since we sat together at dinner, and I see you have not yet learnt to disengage yourself from the trammels of society. You are rather grave and abstracted, and I know you are thinking whether you neglected the proper breadth of smile at Mr. Digby's *plaisanteries,* or whether you did not vouchsafe one finger more than necessary to Mr. Harding, and whether you ought not to have given a more scornful glance at a troublesome acquaintance who pushed himself forward as your neighbour at dinner."

By this time Lucy was recovering from her shyness. She laughed and stopped him by saying, " You shall not invent any other thoughts for me."

" Why?" he interposed, " have I been wrong so far?"

" Not entirely," said Lucy; " and I believe you really are laughing at me for having looked grave at Mr. Digby's witticisms, for I saw that you smiled exactly as he wished and expected."

" Nay!" said George Berkeley; "you are now retorting cruelly upon me; and you have made me really penitent!" and he added, more gravely, " It is one of the sins of what is called society that we become too complaisant—too ready to make ourselves pleasant at the cost at times of countenancing what we despise. An honest contempt for frivolity is less often expressed and betrayed than it ought to be."

" In very young people shyness may cause this fault," said Lucy; "in others, I must say, I think it is inexcusable."

" You are stern in your sense of duty," said George Berkeley.

" Stern! am I?" was Lucy's reply.

" Ah!" said he, with a little amused, admiring look at her sweet face, as she so simply spoke those words, "I have no objection to it! I only wish such sternness could be oftener exercised for our good."

Lord Englefield had his revenge on Mr. Berkeley. He was introduced to Lucy after dinner by Mrs. Walter, and he devoted himself to her with great perseverance during the evening. Mr. Berkeley, it was true, was much occupied in discussing politics with an under-secretary of State, and two or three other men of the party; and if he was watching Lucy at times with some anxiety she did not observe it. Lucy had just discovered that politics were a very proper interest for all educated persons, and she would much have preferred listening to the little knot of clever men, amongst whom Mr. Berkeley was standing, to the *tête-à-tête* with her good-looking, self-satisfied, though agreeable companion.

Mrs. Digby's extreme affection for her as she wished her good night, and saw Lord Englefield's anxiety for Lucy's last word, was no consolation for the wasted evening, but she comforted herself by the hope that there might be more time for gaining political information next day. She was disappointed. Lord Englefield persisted in engrossing her attention, and Mr. Berkeley in talking politics.

And so on for two more days. Mrs. Walter's heart bounded with hopes of a coronet, whilst Lucy began to think Digby Manor rather depressing, when, suddenly, Mr. Berkeley seemed to have tired of politics. He passed most of the following days in talking to Lucy, and she found the air of the place much more exhilarating.

In truth, Lucy's calm, unembarrassed manner, under the decided attentions of a young man whom half the mammas in London were *dying to catch*, had not been lost on Mr. Berkeley ; and when, at length, Lord Englefield had ventured on an expression of interest which served to enlighten Lucy, he had happened to overhear and see what passed; there was a start—a hasty effort to recover herself—and then a quietly cold manner that, whilst it repulsed Lord Englefield, was so perfectly civil that it gave him no plea for complaint.

Lord Englefield left Digby Manor the next day, and Mrs. Crofton sighed, with a tender feeling of concern, as the flourish of the postillion's whip told her he was actually gone! It was rather provoking at that moment to see Lucy's face looking particularly cheerful as she and George Berkeley stood together examining a book of prints.

The visit ended for Mrs. Walter with a reverse,

but for Lucy with so much enjoyment that, as she drove home with her brother and sister-in-law, and passed the high wall, and the old gray chimneys of Hulse House, she could hardly bear to think of the probable contrast between her own happy life and the sad lonely one of the recluse, who so sedulously debarred himself from all interchange of kindness and sympathy with his neighbours. He had no agreeable Mr. Berkeley to drive away depressing fancies, but when sad thoughts came he was given up to battle with them alone.

Mr. Colville had been brought up in all the outward orthodoxy of the Church. Twenty or thirty years ago the exterior of religion was often the utmost that any young man of fashion pretended to, and indifference, or even professed unbelief, was, unhappily, almost the commoner characteristic of the young men of the day. Up to the time of his sorrows, indifference, perhaps, would be the fairest term to give to Arthur Colville's religious views. How indifference darkened into doubt and unbelief, under the pressure of sorrow, I do not wish to relate! As we are introduced to him, on his first coming to Hulse House, his mind was in a gloomy, unsettled misanthropy. It was shaken in every former trust and hope, and it

F 5

is scarcely fair to judge of it as if it were in its chronic, healthy state. Glimpses of it are all I can venture on. The doors of Hulse House were not always open, and I give slight sketches alone, the result of transient peeps through those prison bars.

Amongst his library were many books of deep Divinity. It so chanced that his mind turned for relief, not to the simple truths of revealed religion, which might have given it strength and repose, but to that mass of errors, doubts and subtleties, to be found amongst the mystifications of scholastic theology. Whilst poring about, and turning round and round for occupation in the cramped shell into which his faculties were forced within the walls of Hulse House, he suddenly lighted one day on these abstruse studies.

Unhinged and restless, he was just in the state to love the toilsome work of leaving truth to speculate on the chances of falsehood. Colville read and read—he got deeper into the mire as he went on—he thought, then read; then thought again. The Bible was dragged forth, not to see what *was*, but to search for what was *not* there. If not there, an able commentator proved that it must or should be there. A whole theory hung upon it! Whatever else was wrong, the theory must be right! Another, no less learned commentator, proved that what was clear and evident must be false! Were it not so the truth would stand staring so nakedly before the world that disquisition, logic, argument, all were needless. Now could this be? Forbid it, Heaven!

Arthur Colville was deep amongst these learned philosophers as Hodson opened the door and asked, " Will you ride to-day, sir?" The question was twice repeated.

Mr. Colville stood with a large folio resting on the back of a chair, one hand pressing his forehead, the other holding the book. He read intently, greedily. Hodson stood there with a half smile on his face, for he was pleased that his master had found an interest. He waited some little time. Colville's hand was removed from his forehead—his brain was less perplexed—he turned another page. " Convincing! satisfactory! cannot be a doubt!" were his eager exclamations, and as he looked up to declare to the grave and learned doctors of the contending party, that the dispute was settled, his eye fell on Hodson's civil, respectful face and figure. He looked a moment, passed his hands before his eyes, looked up again, and then, for the first time for many a long sad month, Hodson heard, with joy that did him honour, a short, merry laugh, burst from the lips of his master. "You—you, Hodson! only you! but convincing, nevertheless—convincing, nevertheless!" he repeated, laughing again more heartily.

Hodson smiled—he almost laughed—yet the tears stood in his eyes. It was so long since he had heard that sound! he brushed his hand hastily across his eyes—his heart was full, a throng of recollections came crowding on him; vivid and only too distinct.

Mr. Colville laughed for a time, then suddenly stopped, and looked half suspiciously round. Hodson's face was grave and respectful in a moment. "Will you ride to-day, sir?" he repeated, as if all that we have related—all this tide of emotion—had had no existence.

The effort was rewarded—the look of annoyance that begun to creep over the face of Colville, left it, and he said, carelessly, "Yes, I will ride;" and again he spoke kindly. "These books interest me, Hodson; but as it is fine, I think you may order the horse."

Then looking round as if seeking for something, he laid his hand on a handsomely bound book that was lying on a separate table, and as Hodson was leaving the room, he called him back.

"Here, Hodson," he said, "here is a book that I laid aside for you, when I was arranging my library. You must take it as a present from me. I think you will like it."

Hodson took the book—he bowed low, as he said, "Thank you, sir;" but his voice was husky and his eyes were not raised to his master's face. He left the room quickly. In after times that book, wrapped in its neat cover, was shown to his children's children, a memorial of past kindness, and of attachment that had not passed, though it was then a memory alone.

CHAPTER XII.

The summer and autumn were over: it was early in December, and there could scarcely have been a more dull, cold, unlovely day; but Lucy Crofton did not think so, as she sat in the carriage with her brother Edward on the road to Digby Manor. Mrs. Walter had given Lucy many sisterly cordials before they set out on their visit. She had spoken a good deal about new friends, in a dry cutting way, which implied that even at the age of seventeen it was better to cling resolutely to the past. She hoped Lucy would like her visit! She supposed Mr. Berkeley would not be there, and it could be no matter of regret to any one if he were not, and she begged her not to fancy herself in love with any one who good-naturedly talked to her for ten minutes together.

But these pleasant remarks faded from Lucy's mind under the genial influence of Edward's presence. He was in remarkably good spirits; he had a short holiday from his London work, he liked being with Lucy, and there was something sociable and cheerful in the house at Digby Manor to which they were going. Clever men were apt to be met there, and there was a large library.

"How good these roads are," he said, as they drove quickly along. "The art of road making is improving. Our new railway cuttings bring us back to the idea of the Roman works, with their straight forward way of going to the point, scorning every obstacle. We used to try this in a barbarous stupid way, going up and down for no evident purpose. Just the difference between bravado and courage. There is something grand in the indomitable useful energy of the Romans." And so he went on, and then took up another subject, and he never seemed to think of the Digbys, or Spencers, or himself, till the carriage drove up to the door, and they caught sight of Agnes Spencer's beautiful face as she stood on the terrace watching for them. Lucy thought she looked pale.

"I have been travelling about admiring," Agnes said, as if to apologize for her pale cheeks. "It is very fatiguing and profitless. It is much better to be admired."

"To be admired!" Edward Crofton said, taking up Miss Spencer's words, as if it were an odd new idea. "To be admired! and that is pleasant, is it? It is a sensation I have never tried. To be admired vulgarly and ignorantly, it seems to me would give very little gratification. It ought to be admiration nicely fitted into the interstices of the character."

"No, no!" Agnes exclaimed, "the admiration must be blind, hearty, undiscriminating. I will not be talked down; I will boldly say again, it is pleasant to be admired. There! Mr. Crofton! now answer me, laugh at me, criticize!"

"Nay," said Edward, with his amused smile curling along his lips; "you have disarmed criticism by saying what you know we shall not believe. If indeed you heartily desire to be admired, your wish will probably be gratified; but I cannot promise you only blind admiration."

"And if not blind, it would not proceed from affection!" said Agnes, quickly. "It would arise from a due weighing of merits and virtues—a poor, cold, lifeless thing—admiration such as you would give to a prize cabbage! No, no! I must have blind admiration, warm from the heart, or none!"

"But why not the two together?" said Edward;

but before Agnes had time to answer, he had become abstracted. She turned to Lucy, who was just now disengaged from the affectionate questionings of Mrs. Digby as to the health and happiness of everything that Lucy loved.

"You must come to warm yourself in my room, Lucy," she said, "and let me see whether you are yourself! I never know people till they take off their bonnets, and talk to me over my own fire."

"And how is your wild man of the woods, the man in the cage," Agnes exclaimed, after they had discussed various other subjects together. "Has he peeped through the bars yet, and said, 'Ah, ah! I see it is a merry world enough—pray let me out!'"

Lucy slightly laughed—she could not bear to make a jest of Mr. Colville's unhappiness. "No!" she said; "Mr. Colville is still a recluse."

"Still!" said Agnes. "Has no pretty bird sung on this side the wires and lured him forth; or must some other bird sing sadly, too, in solitude, and echo back his notes! As for me, had I a sorrow such as his may be, I would brave it out in the wide world, and sing with loud and merry notes, till the very rocks and stones should laugh for joy to hear me! Yes, I would brave it out, even though I might hide in those merry notes the aching heart that was ready to break for sadness!" and her voice became sad and low, as if her own heart ached for the one she had pictured to herself, and then turning quickly to Lucy, as if she had worked herself up into a kind of mimic indignation, she said, half angrily and scornfully, "You live so near, and yet you cannot see him! Is this active zeal? Is this kindness and charity? Had I been in your place, long, long before this, I would have seen him! I would have read deep into his heart! Yes," she added, "I would have probed his grief—I would have made him own that others, too, can grieve! I would have brought the sunlight to his sorrow, and bid him say if there were not sorrows as great, or greater, than his, hidden in the heart, and carried about in the world, with a covering of smiles, and jests, and cheerful looks, but lying heavy there—ay, he little knows how heavily!" And thus she had gone on with increasing warmth and earnestness, and then she stopped suddenly; and before Lucy had time to speak, or to explain the impossibility of getting admission to Hulse House, she had flown off to another subject.

"Sadly flighty, indeed," said my sister Martha,

as I paused. "And how did the evening pass, and who were the company?"

"That is precisely what I never was told," said I; "but I am certain that Mr. Fitzgerald must have been staying at Digby Manor, for I have it on record, that one morning Miss Spencer said to him,

"Where is Mr. Edward Crofton?"

"In the library, of course!" was the answer.

"But I want him to walk with us," said Agnes, rather pettishly.

"Shall I tell him so?" Mr. Fitzgerald asked.

"You will not get him," said Lucy.

"Go and try, Mr. Fitzgerald!" Agnes exclaimed, for her spirit immediately rose at the idea of any opposition to her wishes.

He went, with a laughing reproof to Miss Spencer, for being as much spoilt as ever.

"He *must* come!" said Agnes, half wilfully and angrily, when Mr. Fitzgerald had left the room. Lucy shook her head. The door was opening.

"Yes, yes! I knew he would!" Agnes exclaimed. But it was only Mr. Fitzgerald.

"He is much obliged, but he is particularly engaged just now," said Mr. Fitzgerald.

"Oh! you are a poor ambassador!" Agnes

cried out. "I shall go myself. I know I shall bring him;" and she darted off to the library.

"Surely he will come with such a messenger!" said Mr. Fitzgerald; and Lucy heard him sigh as he sat down to look at the little clever pen and ink sketch Agnes had been making.

"You hardly know my brother," Lucy said, "otherwise you would feel as certain as I am that even Miss Spencer will not succeed."

It was some time before Agnes came back, but when she did, it was without Edward.

"Baffled," she said, "completely baffled! Never was there such a failure! There I found him, buried in books, and I went in on tiptoes, and I made myself into a book, and we held a conversation as if we were two volumes; and we went on with such outpouring of knowledge from volume number one, your brother, that volume number two, your humble servant, was almost overwhelmed in the mighty rush of thought; but when volume two tried to back out of it by leading volume one into the next room, a certain well-known smile twinkled out of his eyes, and volume two had to give it up, and come back, Mr. Fitzgerald"— turning archly to him—"disappointed of her whims, as you wish she should be!"

Mr. Fitzgerald smiled at her; but Lucy could

not help noticing the sad expression that followed his smile, as he looked at this winning, fascinating friend, whom he had loved so long and so hopelessly.

"I often wonder," Agnes said, more gravely, "at the power of abstraction which men possess; scarcely any women have it in the same degree. Is it nature or education?"

"A little of both, I should think, said Mr. Fitzgerald. "We are less imaginative, to begin with, and it is necessary for us working men to possess it. The habit begins at school, and must be thoroughly learnt if we would do any good in after life."

"And for us, I know Lucy would say," said Agnes, "that it is necessary to learn to be *sub*tracted, and to be ready to give our attention to any one who wants it, in the midst of our pleasantest occupations."

Lucy smiled. "Yes!" she said; "but I think the habit of thorough attention for the time to one subject is very useful even for us."

"No useless flights into the library and back again!" said Agnes, gaily; and then she went off singing a few notes of a lively French song. But if Miss Spencer's time for serious abstraction had not yet arrived, neither were Lucy's attempts at undivided attention more successful next morning, as she vainly tried to read a little book Mr. Digby had begged her to look at, whilst a conversation was going on between Agnes and Mr. Fitzgerald, of which Mr. George Berkeley was the subject.

"George Berkeley is the most agreeable person I know," said Agnes. "He does not sit studying what to say that will please, but his intelligence and kind nature make him actually blunder on the very words that are most welcome. He has inherited agreeableness and tact from his mother."

"Yes!" said Mr. Fitzgerald; "but what say you to sweet temper and humility?"

"Warmth of heart, at any rate!" said Agnes. "She is the strongest lover I know."

"Yes! and the strongest hater," was the rejoinder.

"Ah, well! I fear so; and the most unreasonable and unreasoning of all clever women, where a fancy seizes her! But with all that, there is something very grand about her character—the fine majestic way in which she sweeps down all obstacles that interfere with her own objects! Her very selfishness has nobleness in it! She would deny herself down to bread and water, and even then would give away the last crust and the last drop of water, to any one whom she loved; and for an object she recognised as worthy she would march boldly on into the blazing fire of martyrdom, if it pleased any one to put it in her way."

"Yes!" said Mr. Fitzgerald; "or pop some other poor wretch in."

"Certainly," said Agnes, laughing, "if they made the obstacle to any scheme for her son's interests. But still she would think she was doing right."

"I should rather pity the bold person who tried to show her she was doing wrong," interposed Mr. Fitzgerald.

"So should I," said Agnes. "I own to her faults; but what a charm there is in her! She is beautiful even now, and her smile is the most irresistible thing I know. How devotedly her sons love her!"

"And obey her!" said Mr. Fitzgerald.

"Yes, indeed!" Agnes said. "George Berkeley loves her so much that he would obey her in everything."

"Even as to his choice of a wife?" said Mr. Fitzgerald.

"Oh, he is too poor to marry!" was Agnes's reply. "But indeed you are right so far, that, owing to a strange legal arrangement of his father's, George is dependent on her in money matters, and he *could* not marry unless his mother gave up part of her income to him. But though George cannot marry, I wonder Frederick does not."

" But where is the lady his mother would think good enough?" said Mr. Fitzgerald, laughing.

This conversation was not soon forgotten by Lucy. Mr. Berkeley's mother became a sort of bugbear to her fancy. If she found herself thinking of Mr. George Berkeley with very agreeable recollection, a vision of a grand, stern, proud woman, with a determined will, and an iron power over her son's affections, accompanied these pleasant remembrances, and she wished she had not happened to listen to that teazing conversation. She turned again very energetically to her book, and tried to be *abstracted*, whilst Edward, Mr. Fitzgerald, and Agnes, slided into a quiet, serious conversation. Mrs. Digby joined them, and presently Agnes started up, and said,

" How grave we have all become! Mrs. Digby, may we have some music?" then turning towards Mr. Fitzgerald, she said, " Why are people ever grave? I hate gravity!"

" You don't do yourself justice," said Mr. Fitzgerald. "I know no one who is able to be grave with so much grace."

Miss Spencer half smiled, and then looked sad, but she said, lightly enough, "In spite of that pretty compliment, Mr. Fitzgerald, I am determined to repeat that I hate gravity."

Edward Crofton was looking earnestly at her. She happened to perceive it.

"Mr. Crofton," she said, "I see you are preparing to pounce down upon me with some wise saw in praise of solemnity, and to prevent your doing so, I shall go and sing the liveliest song I can find—for I won't be grave, I won't be wise!"

Edward Crofton said hastily, as he stood close to her, so that no one heard but herself, "Who could wish you to change in anything—to be different in the slightest degree from what you are!"

A bright blush crimsoned Agnes Spencer's face. She said no more, but was busy finding her music, and she and Lucy sang some duets together.

CHAPTER XIII.

It is not my object to write a journal of Lucy Crofton's and Agnes Spencer's lives, but merely to note down the incidents or the conversations that tend to develop their characters, or to bring out the plot of their life's story, that wonderful drama each human being enacts or passively passes through—full of interest and strange complexities, no doubt, if we could see the whole, in its completeness, from life to death, however seemingly common-place the events or the characters. And so I silently pass over the next few days at Digby Manor; leaving the degree of intimacy they caused between Miss Spencer and the two Croftons to be imagined by the reader; and whilst Edward Crofton travels back to London, I return, with Lucy, to the Parsonage,—and there we find Mrs. Walter Crofton in a state of unusual excitement.

Two days ago, a groom, on horseback, had been seen dashing at a quick pace along the road leading from Hulse House to the village; the spirited horse was foaming and chafing with the unwonted exercise, whilst the groom had an air of importance, as much as to say that at last his master was condescending to notice his neighbours, although he was much too grand to do so in an habitual and commonplace way. The livery, no doubt, was Mr. Colville's. The village was duly excited, one good wife after another came out at her door, the little boys shouted, the girls screeched, the labourers paused in their work —" the Squire's servant sure enough," was their shrewd remark. Eager faces watched which way the horse would turn—the lane was passed, leading to the neighbouring town, and on he went. It was no medical advice that was required by the Master of Hulse; on, on he still went—the road to the Parsonage was neared—now, would he turn in, or would he not? Yes, yes—he does! he does! And true indeed, the groom hastened to the Parsonage, rang the bell, smiled, in a dignified manner, at the surprised looks of the servants, and drawing a letter from his pocket, neatly folded, sealed, and directed, gave it to Mr. Crofton's footman, and said that he was ordered to wait for an answer.

We must follow the letter to the drawing-room.

The servant took it breathlessly to Mrs. Crofton, Walter being out of doors.

"A letter! Who from?"

The servant, delighted with the importance of the answer he had to give, said, with an attempted air of unconcern—"The letter is from Mr. Colville ma'am!—Mr. Colville, of Hulse House! and the servant waits for an answer."

"Mr. Colville!" was Mrs. Walter's exclamation. "Mr. Colville?"

The servant felt proudly satisfied that the excitement of the news was as much as could be expected.

"Mr. Colville! Run, James! Run and fetch your master! He is only in the village. Give me the letter. Yes, indeed; I thought it would come! Written at last!" Mrs. Walter paused, and examined the outside of the letter—"'The Rev. W. Crofton,' a good firm hand. Well, Mr. Crofton, here it is!" she exclaimed, in an exulting tone, as Walter came in. "Here it is! I told you, sooner or later, it would come."

"What would come?" said Walter, to whom the servant had only announced mysteriously that Mrs. Crofton had a letter for him. "Is it the parcel of books from London? Are they unpacked?"

"Unpacked!" exclaimed Mrs. Walter. "Parcel of books! What can you be thinking of? Here is a letter from Hulse House—from Mr. Colville! His own writing! Open it directly, Walter, and let us hear no more about books."

Even Walter looked surprised and interested. He read the short letter. It was merely a civil request that Mr. Crofton would come and see him.

"I will go at once," said Walter; "who knows what good may be done?" He was putting the letter into his pocket and preparing to set out, forgetting poor Mrs. Walter's eager curiosity, till she screamed out her desire to see it.

"'Mr. Colville's compliments,'" read out Mrs. Walter. "Yes! he sends compliments just like any other man! 'Would feel much obliged.' Why yes, certainly! he might have asked us to dinner, instead of asking to see you as if you were the parish doctor or attorney."

"Or parish priest which I am," said Walter. "And I am glad he sends for me. It has been on my conscience that my richest parishioner might need my help more than the poorest in my charge."

"You will just notice a little, Walter," said Mrs. Crofton, anxiously, as Walter took up his hat to go; "you will just notice a little how the rooms are furnished, and whether there are many pretty knick-knacks lying about, and how many servants. These little things, you know, tell a great deal; open your eyes for once, Walter, instead of walking on as if you were blind, as you generally do; and just look if he......"

Here Mrs. Walter's injunctions became useless, by Walter's shutting the door after him as he left the room.

As Walter Crofton paced along the road, for his first interview with Arthur Colville, he felt a more serious, and even inquisitive, interest than he let his wife perceive. Sometimes, as he went, he half laughed at himself for the gravity of his views, and the supposition that this visit should lead to any serious results. Mr. Colville's might be a simple act of tardy civility, and the visit might prove as formal and uninteresting as any other to a mere country neighbour. He reached Hulse, and was shown into the library. As the servant ushered him in, a tall, pale, handsome young man came forward to meet him. There was a strong and touching interest to Walter, as he found himself, for the first time, in the presence of the mysterious recluse of Hulse House, and his eyes first rested on his face, and the tones of his voice first sounded in his ears—

"I sincerely thank you, Mr. Crofton, for your readiness in attending to my request," were his words, as he extended his hand to Walter.

Arthur Colville had that air of refinement and high breeding which is not a common gift, and which, if not bestowed by nature, can rarely, if ever, be acquired. He was tall, but stooped a little. His eye was keen, but melancholy; and there was a slightly peevish or satirical expression in the lower part of his face. In speaking to Walter he scarcely seemed to look at him, as if careless as to any sympathy or interchange of feeling; but rather, on the contrary, proudly defiant of any personal interest or communion with his visitor. The ordinary modulation of his voice was low and gentle, but every now and then it was raised with a slightly fretful intonation. There was something striking and unusual in his whole look and manner, at once creating a feeling of interest and pity, which feeling he seemed utterly to reject and despise.

"I asked you to come here, Mr. Crofton," he said, "in defiance of the usual forms of society.

But it is better to break through these forms, and to enter at once on our subject, instead of toiling through the brick and mortar, and iron—yes, the *iron* of social etiquette."

His voice became querulous as he spoke; unused as he was to an auditor, Mr. Colville, perhaps, had almost forgotten that he had one now.

"And so, Mr. Crofton," he continued, "you will kindly let me break through these barriers, and go to the point at once. I am alone," he said, after a slight pause—and there was something in his way of saying those words, that made Walter again raise his eyes, with strong interest, to Mr. Colville's face. It was slightly agitated; no doubt, from expressing for the first time, and to a stranger, the entire loneliness of his existence. "I am alone," he repeated, in a low, touching voice, as though the words had betrayed to his own heart the sadness of his solitude, and as if he were almost answering a doubt from his hearer that such a miserable lot could really be his; but although his eye never sought that of Walter's, he seemed to divine that he was pitying him; there was no start, no very evident sign of annoyance, but he continued his sentence in an entirely different tone.

"And thus I am able to read and think more

than others," he added. "These books are excellent companions," laying his hand on some large ones, lying on his table, "but they are a little abstruse—perhaps to many more bewildering than useful." His voice was rising to its more querulous pitch. "The deep mysteries of philosophy and of nature, of which they treat, are to me, I own, an exercise and a delight. But whilst these writers possess the skill to suggest difficulties and to raise doubts, most clearly and ably"—he stopped a moment, and then added, drily and ironically—"they have omitted to give us the answers, Mr. Crofton. The answers to all these doubts are omitted!—and this is my reason for wishing to talk with you. Books may, at times, be better than living commentators; but there are cases in which questions arise to which there is no written answer. Two minds are better than one: especially where the one"—slightly bowing to Walter—"is, no doubt, more clear—more amply stored than the other. It would please me much, if you could occasionally spare time enough to discuss with me some of these abstruse questions. I have a good library, there are works that would interest you; some, I believe, are difficult to procure. Could you occasionally come for an hour to try with me the merits of these learned men?"

Walter was, in truth, much given to the abstruse reading in which Arthur Colville was immersed. He said that an excuse for such studies was particularly agreeable to him.

"Then let us begin at once," said Colville, and with the eagerness of a spoilt child he seated himself at the table where his books lay, and opening at various marked passages, he gave Walter a rapid and masterly sketch of the points in question, and soon both Mr. Colville and Walter Crofton were so deeply engaged that they forgot the hour—forgot that they were entire strangers to one another; Mr. Colville forgot that he was a recluse—Walter, that the being he talked with was the strange unknown, who had shunned his very sight till that moment.

When Walter Crofton returned home, at the end of some hours' time, he could laugh heartily at his wife's tender anxiety on his account: anxiety which had led her to suppose more than once that the mad solitary had stabbed or imprisoned her poor husband within the gloomy walls of Hulse House; anxiety that led her to scold all the servants by way of passing the time; and anxiety that finally made her set out on the road leading to

Hulse House, from whence she might at least have the melancholy satisfaction of hearing the stifled groans of her murdered husband.

The sight of Walter, quietly trudging along, or sometimes pausing to peep into a book which he was carrying, relieved her anxieties, and his hearty laugh, as she told him what she had suffered for his sake, so far reassured her that she was able to be rather angry at his indifference.

"A very agreeable, gentlemanlike man," said Walter. "He shows much learning; and, if he would only do it in moderation, he is none the worse for giving up society and living entirely in as fine a library as I ever beheld."

"Oak?" asked Mrs. Walter, eagerly, "with crimson damask and fine pictures?"

"Oh! as to that," said Walter, "I really don't know. I meant the books—a most valuable and curious collection!"

Mrs. Walter gave a contemptuous "*hem!*" but was too eager to hear all that Walter could tell to express her contempt at the moment. "And did he ask us to dinner?"

"No," said Walter.

"Strange, indeed!" said Mrs. Walter. "It would have been more civil — but perhaps to breakfast or luncheon?"

"No indeed; he said nothing about eating."

"But, no doubt, he said something about me! Some little curiosity, I should think, as to what *my* opinion of him might be!"

Walter smiled. "Indeed, my dear, he seemed very easy on that subject, for he never even named you. I doubt whether he knows if I am married or single."

"Oh! indeed!" said Mrs. Walter, with a slight toss of the head, "it is very well for him to make believe he don't care to know, but depend upon it he knew all about us long before he sent for you, and I dare say was quite aware of Lucy's absence before he ventured to do so, thinking how likely the neighbourhood would be to gossip. Did he inquire when Lucy would return?"

"My dear, I told you before that he never named either you or Lucy. We talked of books, and books only."

"An interesting subject, truly!" said Mrs. Walter, indignantly. "A set of old dusty lumber! no gentleman would ever devote his whole time to such useless trash!"

Mrs. Walter could gain no more explicit information in answer to her many questions, and she ended by protesting that she should consider it a sad waste of time for her husband ever to set his foot in Hulse House again, and that, for her part, she had not the slightest wish to see so stupid, and evidently illbred a person as Mr. Colville. As each time she expressed this sentiment to Walter, he told her that he saw no reason to fear she should ever be put to the test, she had nothing to do but loudly to re-echo her assertion, whilst devising every scheme in her power to bring about a meeting.

In answer to a question from my sister Martha, at this crisis, I answered that Walter Crofton was not at present aware of any religious infidelity on Mr. Colville's part.

CHAPTER XIV.

MANY months have rolled away. Hulse House is again a silent mystery. Mrs. Walter had wondered and wondered, till even her wondering ceased, there was so little food on which to keep her curiosity alive. These months had rolled on quickly or slowly, as different minds had viewed them; to the young they were large vast periods of a life that looked to them interminable in the far-off future of new interests, which were then springing up so thickly around them that they believed they would continue to do so for ever. To the old—ah! how short and unexciting these months appeared, as they noiselessly rushed by with ever-increasing velocity, leaving less and less of a future of hope or of novelty to look to in this world, but to many, let me add, even more of peace and happiness and rational enjoyment.

Now I am old, I can hardly understand the intensity of interest of which youth is capable as to passing events, and yet I would not have their eagerness or their enthusiasm lessened. It is all in its place, and there would be a kind of moral morass into which everything would sink if it were not so. I am settled down into the vale of years, but I delight to know that there are young spirits gaining freshness and vigour from the exhilarating air on the mountain tops.

I think Lucy Crofton had a good many of these pleasant breezes fanning her cheeks during the last few months, and some sterner gales between times to brace up her powers for the conflict of life. As to Hulse House, its owner seemed sinking deeper and deeper into that morass of hopelessness of which I have spoken—there was youth, indeed, but no youthful enthusiasm.

In one of my usual summer exploring expeditions, I went to look at Hillesden, the family seat of the Spencers. There is a remarkably handsome avenue, reaching nearly to the house. I liked riding slowly along it, knowing that the high spirited Agnes Spencer, about whom I was becoming greatly interested, had often galloped along it on her pony as a child, full of glee and enjoyment, and before I saw it, I knew that my dear little Lucy Crofton had walked under those fine arching elms, the flickering light and shade from their waving branches had played upon her pretty face, and those old stately trees had heard the sweet tones of her voice, as she and Agnes paced up and down with plenty of light and shade falling on them both morally and physically.

Lucy and Edward Crofton had each of them visited Hillesden, but I have not been able to get any particulars of this period of their history, and I shall perhaps surprise the reader as much as I myself was surprised when, after some difficulty, I puzzled out the fact that Edward Crofton was so much attracted by Miss Spencer that he at length ventured to express his admiration to her. No one will suppose that such a man would act presumptuously, and I cannot clearly discover the reasons why he gave utterance to a love which he, in his peculiarly humble, modest nature, scarcely dreamt would be returned. All I know is that the avowal did not lessen Miss Spencer's respect for his character, or weaken her love for his sister.

She had, in truth, singularly appreciated him, and but for a strong pre-engagement of her affections, there was little doubt he would not have spoken in vain.

Lucy was the only confidante, but after the first agitated avowal, which circumstances rather drew from him, the subject was entirely dropped between Edward and herself.

"Ah, Lucy!" Agnes said one day to her, after a long reverie consequent on a letter Lucy had just received from her brother. "Ah! Lucy!" but for that terrible past how happy we all three might have been!"

Lucy dared not utter what was almost at her heart to say—"And is there still no hope!" for she saw that any allusion to the possibility of her forming a new attachment was the cause of great and very painful agitation to Agnes.

I stopped reading at this juncture.

"It is a pity she could not love him!" said my sister Jane, quietly, "he was such a good man, and so clever too! But marriages are made in Heaven, they say, and no doubt there is some good wife in store for him!"

"Jane!" said my sister Martha, reproachfully, with a side glance at me, which it was supposed I did not see.

The reader will scarcely need to be told that I am an old bachelor; but in spite of the implied wound to my feelings, I resumed my reading with unruffled composure, though my sister Jane fidgetted and got red, and blew her nose several times in an agitated manner as I proceeded.

Edward Crofton was not the sort of person who would speak of his feelings, or give way to a morbid indulgence of useless sorrow; and I could learn nothing about him for a long interval, but that after awhile he wrote cheerful business-like political letters to the parsonage. He was evidently determined to make the hard, stirring interests of life obliterate the short, sweet, yet troubled recollections that clung round Digby Manor and Hillesden; but some of us may guess that there were hours when these memories would pertinaceously intrude into the deepest study, and that even Edward Crofton, with his strong, calm nature, seemed to himself weak as a child, when any accidental circumstance brought to his mind the thought of Agnes Spencer, and of that first delightful dawn of the tender, unselfish affection, which, perhaps, few men can feel but once in their lives.

CHAPTER XV.

THE law of chance is one of the strange enigmas which my sisters, Martha and Jane, obstinately refuse to believe. If it is chance they say it is not a law. I state, as a fact, one of those curious chances that elderly females love to look on as miracles.

Late in the summer, Lucy Crofton went to pay a long-deferred visit to Mr. and Mrs. Wilton, who had been friends of her father's, at their beautiful place at Fernmere, upon one of our English Lakes. Mr. Berkeley and his brother George rented a small fishing and shooting cottage close to the Wiltons; and this year George Berkely *chanced* to visit it without his brother, and when Lucy arrived at Fernmere the first person she heard spoken of was George Berkeley. With what a pretty flush of pleased surprise this name was listened to by her, I will not tell—nor how the summer days flew by at that beautiful Fernmere—amongst the cheerful, happy family party of the Wiltons, with George Berkeley as their constant guest.

It is more than a year since I first spoke of Lucy Crofton as she sat watching the red and yellow tulips, lighted up by the sunshine, from the bay-window of the Parsonage, and now the sun shines brightly on a gorgeous group of crimson, and purple, and amber-coloured dahlias, in the garden of Fernmere, and it then falls with a softer light through the open window on Lucy's face as she looks up with half-breathless pleased attention to Mrs. Henry Wilton and George Berkeley, who are talking together. George Berkeley has been speaking on subjects of deep interest, and Lucy begins to feel that he has a way of expressing himself, and a tone of thought that are, to her fancy, more perfect than that of any other human being. And yet! little, happy, self-deceiving Lucy, she does not dream of love! she thinks that that solemn, serious incident in her life is still far off! No fond aunt, no older sister, no gossiping maid has talked to her about it, and it is still to her a sacred thing, a subject on which she believes that none would speak lightly but the frivolous or unrefined, the coarse or vulgar.

But this pretty and perilous era in her girlhood is opening on her; and now that she is happy in its first untroubled approaches, I will return to that gloomy gray house which she left behind her, looking as melancholy as ever. This last year that has been to Lucy Crofton one of pleasant variety and new interests, has dragged on in weary length to the prisoner at Hulse House. Neither Walter Crofton nor even Lucy herself could half imagine the utter dreariness of Arthur Colville's mind, during the intervals of Walter's visits. How often had that high park wall seen the solitary rider on the one dull, shadowy side, and the busy, cheerful, useful numbers on the gay, sunny side as those months wore away!

Mr. Colville had not dared to send for Walter Crofton again, after two or three visits had passed, for he was afraid of becoming too much used to companionship. He was not pleased to find that his mind was insufficient to itself, and his very cheerfulness in Walter's society vexed him. It was but cheerfulness for the moment, and it somehow lowered the grandeur of his sorrow in his own eyes, and he therefore let himself sink again into his habitual, morose, bitter misanthropy.

However, after some months, his longing to see Walter returned in such force that he penned another note, asking him to come and resume their literary pursuits. He paced up and down the broad terraced gravel-walk before the windows, as the servant rode off with the note, and he smiled faintly as the thought of Walter Crofton's visit gave him some object to look to in the coming day.

"Your brother has at last seen Mr. Colville again," Mrs. Walter wrote to Lucy at Fernmere; "and he came home in good spirits from the interview; but for my part I can see no good in his passing half the morning cramming his brain with a parcel of old-fashioned notions, just for the sake of proving that nobody knows anything. If Walter gets these ideas put into his head we shall have him refusing to preach soon, unless he can prove that two and three make four; and whatever he may say, I will never believe that Mr. Colville is *a gentleman*, till he invites us all to dinner to meet a pleasant party of his country neighbours."

CHAPTER XVI.

As I said before, this story is not to be a journal of Lucy Crofton's and Agnes Spencer's lives. I merely note down the events that are of importance to either of them.

A year has passed since I last spoke of Lucy Crofton. She is again on a visit to the Wiltons at Fernmere. The day is a calm August day. The lake sleeps placidly, and the little boat is prepared for an expedition to the other side; and on the other side there are to be numberless pleasures—sketching, and reading, and climbing mountains. The day is perfect, and so is Lucy, in her simple country dress; and George Berkeley helps her into the boat, and Mr. and Mrs. Wilton, and their daughter-in-law, and their young cousin, and their grandchildren, make up the party.

"Only a month, only a month left!" sighed forth little Charlie Wilton. "But perhaps we shall all stay longer! perhaps, Miss Lucy, you will! mamma and everybody will be so glad!"

"Only a month left!" was echoed in Lucy's heart. But she said aloud, "No, no! Charlie; I have been here too long already!"

George Berkeley looked at her. Surely her voice was sad! Yes, it was sad! Lucy knew now that she loved George Berkeley, and she believed that her love was unreturned. Her womanly dignity made her shrink with distress from this conviction, and every effort must be made to conceal her secret. She thought, with sensitive annoyance, that Mr. Berkeley had noticed those few words, she had so weakly uttered, but she determined that he should not discern any more sadness, and whilst he walked a little way apart with the pale Clara Wilton, the young cousin of the Wiltons, no one seemed more happy than Lucy, as she was surrounded by the merry group of children. But when the children ran off on a message to their mamma, she seated herself on some rocks on the mountain side that she might look at the scene beneath which was beautiful. Her eye rested on it in pleased admiration, till it turned to another object. Not far off stood George Berkeley, whilst Clara Wilton rested on the grass. She looked very calm, and statue-like, and lovely, and George Berkeley watched her, and helped her to rise, as she languidly got up, and he was speaking to her—Lucy hardly knew how—tenderly, or how was it? She could not tell, but her eyes were moist with tears. Clara Wilton was an orphan like herself. She was grave, and sad, and quiet, but strangely reserved. Lucy liked her, but she could not fathom her reserve; but there was one person who seemed to have done so—and that was George Berkeley! Lucy had seen it now for many days. Last year, when she was with the Wiltons, Mr. Berkeley was there also, but Clara Wilton was away. It had been different then; yes, very different! Lucy sighed. She saw clearly now why that difference made her unhappy. Yes, it was a death-blow to her happiness, but she must not show that it was; least of all must George Berkeley see it, and so her laugh was again heard, as the children rejoined her. And when the lengthening shadows told them that this day of pleasure was ended, and they stepped once more into the boat that was to take them back to the other side the lake, none seemed gayer than Lucy; and the children said,

"Oh, grandpapa! do let us have another merry day across the lake, with dear Miss Crofton!"

and Lucy almost shuddered, as she sat in the boat in the calm evening time, at the thought of *such* another merry day! How could she bear it?

The next morning, she had escaped from all the party, and was wandering alone through the wood that edged the lake, and George Berkeley and Clara Wilton were in her thoughts. Soon they were not in her thoughts alone—she heard their voices, she saw them in a distant bend of the road. She returned to the house. Must she indeed stay here this long, long month? Can she not possibly persuade her sister, or Walter, to order her home before the allotted two months' visit to the Wiltons is over? or must she stay to watch, day by day, the growth of George Berkeley's love, and wait to hear the announcement, and to join in the congratulations?

"You have tired yourself," said grandmamma Wilton, who was matter-of-fact; "go and lie down my dear, and rest till we call for you."

Lucy obeyed. She was very weary, and she owned it.

The days wore on, Lucy scarcely knew how. Constantly before her was the consciousness of a secret understanding between Mr. Berkeley and Clara Wilton. What did it matter to Lucy that he often devoted himself more than ever to her; that he often tried to remind her of words and events during that last happy year at Fernmere; that he often asked her to sing again the songs he had first heard at Digby Manor? What was it when there was the secret glance, the half-whispered word, to that calm, passionless Clara Wilton, bringing up the faint blush on her pale statue-like face? No, no! Lucy felt she must go home, and forget him; and she even counted the days and the hours, till she should be released from the constant pain of seeing him and Miss Wilton together.

But this pain was unexpectedly shortened. Clara Wilton was summoned away a week before Lucy was to return home.

CHAPTER XVII.

BEFORE I say any more of Lucy Crofton, and observe how she bears this new trouble in her life, I must change the scene.

A lady, apparently a foreigner, is travelling with her maid, to visit some of the beautiful scenery in the north of England. The day was drawing to a close when the carriage reached the lodge gates of Cleveland. The lady eagerly looked out of the window, and called to the driver, in broken English, to stop, as the carriage was wheeling past the lodge. The driver pulled up his horses.

"Madame la Comtesse wished to see the grounds," the maid said, in English, to the driver. "She would walk from thence whilst the carriage waited outside the lodge gates."

"*Depechez vous*," exclaimed the lady, in an impatient tone, as the driver came to open the carriage door.

"My lady bids you be quick," said the maid; but before the steps were half down, her mistress had sprung out.

The lady's companion slowly followed, whilst Madame la Comtesse, half ran forward in her eagerness to look at the place, of whose beauty she had heard a flaming account at the neighbouring town.

When a little way out of sight of the lodge, she at times slackened her pace, or even stood quite still, then again started on, as if impatient to reach some desired point of view, and, at last, on gaining a little knoll under a tree, she threw herself on the grass, and the tears trickled fast through the slender fingers which were pressed over her eyes. Then she again eagerly raised her head, looked around her as if to make herself thoroughly acquainted with the scene, and again started up and proceeded on her way, till she came in sight of the house. She then walked leisurely on till her maid joined her. They reached the front door, and rang the bell. The lady started violently as the door was opened, but she soon regained the well-bred, rather patronizing manner of society, which seemed natural to her.

The housekeeper was called, and they proceeded to see the house. The Comtesse talked incessantly as she walked through the rooms, and if the housekeeper, perplexed by her foreign idiom, lost her meaning, the lady applied to her companion to explain. She turned away with indifference from what were called the state rooms—probably feeling their inferiority to the palaces of nobles on the continent—but she seemed to delight to linger in those which the housekeeper told her had been in daily use.

In one of these there was an admirable portrait. The housekeeper had just followed the Comtesse into the room, as her eye first caught sight of this picture, when suddenly she heard her exclaim, in a tone of deep emotion, as she started back and clasped her hands before her eyes,

"Oh! my God! it is himself!"

The housekeeper stared at her, and the Comtesse at length observing her look of surprise, with a return of her lively French manner, said,

"This picture remind me of one old friend I do often think upon. Perhaps it may be your noble milord's *charmant* son?"

"It is my master himself!" said the housekeeper, with much important pride.

"Ah! *qu'il est beau!* How noble! I must sit and look one leetle more. *Pardonne!* You,

Sophie, go on, whilst I rest here," and so saying, she seated herself opposite the picture, whilst the others went on to the next room, her companion explaining to the housekeeper that her lady loved pictures very much, and possessed some fine ones of her own.

There sat the Comtesse mean time, her eyes riveted on this beautiful work of art. But, no! it was not its artistic merits which engaged her attention.

"'Tis he! 'tis himself!" she exclaimed again; "oh! why, why did I come? Oh! how can I bear it! how can I bear it?"

She bent down and covered her face; then again raised her head and gazed with looks of unspeakable tenderness on the image before her, as if she were striving to imagine life and feeling in the lifeless, soulless portrait. The sound of voices roused her. She hastily wiped her eyes; and when Sophie returned with the housekeeper, she was ready to exclaim, with French liveliness, " how *charmant!* How sad that she must tear herself away! But, *ou est-il?*—where is he, this *aimable jeune homme?*" asked she, pointing to the picture, but not looking at it.

The housekeeper answered that her master was

abroad. The lady turned with a quick and scrutinizing look towards her.

"Abroad!" she exclaimed. "Are you sure?"

"Indeed, my lady, it is surprising, and I am not astonished your ladyship should exclaim at it, with such a place as this as his home; but he has left us for some years."

The lady's astonishment had vanished, it seemed, for she said nothing for a few minutes, but when again walking by the side of their guide she resumed her lively, eager questioning, and seemed to amuse herself in probing the housekeeper's evident attachment and admiration for her master, whilst the housekeeper seemed half pleased and half suspicious at her inquisitiveness.

"*A present*, Sophie, we must go," said she at length to her companion.

She then thanked the housekeeper with great civility for her attention, dropped a handsome present into her hand, and left the house. Not a word did she utter to the attendant, Sophie. They reached the carriage—they got in—the lady threw herself back—still without uttering a word. Sophie gave the direction to the driver, to proceed to the neighbouring town, where they were to pass the night, and the carriage whirled quickly away.

I have related this little incident because we shall see this lady again, and she is intimately connected with the events of my story. I must now go back to Fernmere.

CHAPTER XVIII.

THE last day of Miss Wilton's stay was come. Lucy did not wish to see the parting; having said good-bye herself, she strolled out into the rocky pleasure-ground, with a book in her hand, that she might sit out and read, and as she read, forget the parting that would soon be taking place.

She had seated herself on a grassy knoll, surrounded by jutting rocks, fancifully shaped thorns, mountain ash, and clumps of heather, where she could see the calm, clear lake beneath her— that lake on which she and the children had so often rowed about with Mr. Berkeley in the past year—where this year there had been days of strange, startling pleasure, even when Clara Wilton was present.

It would have been better for Lucy not to watch those little gliding boats, if she wished to forget, and she had just taken up her book and began to read, when she heard voices from the path below. It was one way, but a circuitous one to the carriage road, which led away from Fernmere Hall. She was out of sight, but she knew that the path came close beneath where she was sitting, and before she had time to stir, the speakers were directly underneath. She was paralysed by the confirmation of her heart-sickening fancy before she left the house—that George Berkeley had intended to take this last walk with Miss Wilton, and the first distinct words that reached her ears were those from George Berkeley, which confirmed every fear.

"My mother is very affectionate. She loves her sons. She will not refuse her consent when she knows you better."

Lucy had heard enough; but she dared not move, and the speakers were standing still. No wonder that Clara Wilton was obliged to pause before she could reply to words spoken with such deep earnestness. Had Lucy not been a very unwilling eavesdropper the proverb concerning them would have been falsified in her case, as the next words in Clara Wilton's clear voice fell on her ear.

"And, though my heart might break, I never would marry Frederic without her consent!" was said distinctly and firmly.

"I honour you!" was the quick, enthusiastic reply from George Berkeley, and there was silence for a few minutes, as the speakers passed on, leaving their secret in Lucy's power. When they were gone quite away, Lucy flew, rather than ran to the house. She gained her own room, and locked the door, that she might hide herself even almost from herself, in the exuberance of her joy. I need not try to describe it. Any one who has loved—who has watched as she believed the growth of an attachment to another —and then has suddenly discovered this other to be a friend, instead of a rival, can understand Lucy Crofton's feelings at that moment. She had been struggling bravely against her love, and we may reverence the intensity of her joy, even though she shows the usual womanly sign of it, by bursting into a flood of tears.

But when the first ectasy of this self-indulgence was past, Lucy came to the perplexing question what to do with her secret. She could not *un*know it if she wished, and to wish it unknown— that was impossible! There never was a secret that brought such a warm glow of comfort to her heart! Still there it was—an awkward, dishonourable secret, possessed, as it was, without the rightful owners' knowledge; and how could Lucy give it back to them? Clara Wilton was gone, there was but Mr. Berkeley left.

Lucy looked very sedate, as she sat in the drawing-room next morning, with only Mr. Berkeley in the room, and she raised her head with a determined air, and placed her hands firmly one over the other, as she began to say, "Mr. Berkeley."

George Berkeley slightly started, for somehow it had of late been very unusual for Lucy to address him.

"Mr. Berkeley," Lucy began, and she spoke with great precision, as if determined that he should attend, "I happened yesterday to be in the rock walk when you and Miss Wilton passed by, and I unfortunately overheard a part of your conversation relating to your brother and Miss Wilton. I may be foolish in telling you this, but there seems to me something treacherous in concealing it. If my honesty gives you needless annoyance I hope you will forgive me; but you will, I trust, think of me as if I had not so unluckily been forced into your confidence;" and she got up and was leaving the room, in a quiet, self-possessed way, resolved that Mr. Berkeley should not have the slightest ground for supposing that she sought for farther confidence, or wished to create an interest in him by her confession.

She did not see the expression of admiration that beamed forth on his face as she finished speaking. And yet he did not know half the cause there was for admiration. He did not know —how should he?—what an effect those words had had on Lucy! He did not know the extreme difficulty to her of telling calmly that which had stirred her whole soul to hear! Telling it to him too, for whose sake it had so much affected her! But he saw enough to raise his wondering approval! What a nice sense of honour; what a modest, firm propriety of demeanour were blended with Lucy's peculiar charm of feminine softness! He would not wound her delicacy by word or look that could seem to take advantage of the awkwardness of the disclosure she had had to make. He said, in a manner as quiet and unloverlike as he could assume—

"I have to thank you for acting towards us with your usual delicacy and kindness. I know that my brother's secret is as safe with you as with ourselves, and my only regret is that this accident should have given you a moment's uneasiness," and, as he opened the door for her, he did not try to detain her, and Lucy left the room with his quiet, respectful thanks sounding in her ears.

She had seldom felt more happy. She had got

through a very awkward confession; she was just relieved from an uncomfortable sensation of jealousy, and, to crown all, she had a week longer to stay at Fernmere.

When the children ran to her door, entreating her to come and help them in some of their games of play, she was only too glad to join them, and to have any outlet for her gaiety of heart; and, as she played at battledore and shuttlecock with little Mary Wilton on the lawn, there was a good deal of the joyousness of childhood about her, added to that soft, dignified grace which never for a moment forsook her, let her be as playful and merry as she might.

And George Berkeley, too, was not an unpleasing sight, as he stood there for an instant with his arms folded, his waving hair slightly blown from his forehead, and his eyes fixed on Lucy. Little Annie Wilton, who was just three years old, was much of this opinion, for the moment she saw him, she began to toddle up to him as fast as she could.

"Annie tired," she said; "Annie *so* tired! O carry Annie, dear Mr. Geordy!" and with both her little fat arms she tried to pull him down, till the easier process was effected of lifting her up; and she was soon nestled cosily against his head, as she sat in the place of honour upon his shoulder, with a contented proud smile dimpling up her mouth, as her eyes looked consequentially down on the pigmies below.

CHAPTER XIX.

An odd chance was again at work, when that evening Mrs. Henry Wilton said to George Berkeley, " You know Lord Englefield, I think."

Lucy was sitting almost opposite, at the table round which the party usually congregated in the evening. She saw his quick glance at her, and in her anxiety to appear indifferent, of course she blushed.

" I don't know Lord Englefield very well, but I have a kind of interest about him," he said.

Mrs. Wilton went on, " Some friends of ours are staying with him in the country, and they are full of the charms of his place, and of himself, but they are sadly vexed he does not marry. It would be so desirable for a young man in his position to settle early in life, and he seems not to have the slightest inclination that way."

" Ah!" said Mr. Berkeley, rather bitterly; "it

is but one case out of a hundred. If a young man has every inducement open to him to marry, nothing will persuade him to do so. In spite of the earnest wishes of his friends, he dawdles on, living a selfish, unloving life."

"You speak bitterly," said Mrs. Henry Wilton.

"Yes, I know I do!" was the answer, "for I feel bitterly. If, like me, you were a poor younger son, and those words, 'too poor to marry,' had been dinned into your ears as they have into mine, you would understand a little of my indignation, when I see a person despising the blessing that I know too well how to value."

George Berkeley was silent. Lucy's heart beat fast—she could not look up—she was diligently shading a bit of background in her drawing.

Mr. Wilton spoke next: "I agree with you, Berkeley," he said. "I am not a violent radical, but I should like to invent a law for equality of means amongst the young men of society who won't and who can't marry. Lord Englefield should be made to pay a handsome per centage to those who amiably desire to settle down and give up the best London dinners for moderate ones at home. Some skill would be required to adjust the law."

"My dear," said Mrs. Wilton grandmamma, "how can you wish to encourage imprudent marriages. I think it much better for young people to wait some years."

"Yes, my dear!" said Mr. Wilton; "but the question is, how many years?"

"Yes!" said George Berkeley, gravely; "how many? How many of the best years of a man's life are to be spent in waiting? that is, in gaining selfish habits and modes of thought, that unfit him at length for the duties as well as for the happiness of married life! How seldom can he resist the insiduous influence of the enervating, debasing life of self-indulgence and easily attained luxury, free from home ties and home responsibilities, which is led by him, in common with most young men in the higher classes in society— and it is of them I am now speaking. The woman he loved in his youth sees him becoming day by day less worthy of her love, and less able to contend with the sacrifices a home of poverty must entail upon him. She waits for him—she would sacrifice every luxury for him—but he has learnt to think cautiously; the maxims so sedulously taught him in his frank, joyous youth, are learnt too well, and he ceases even to wish to give up his habitual luxuries for the sake of affection which he has outlived."

George Berkeley paused.

Mr. Wilton spoke. "This is indeed a sadly true view of the case," he said. "I could name several instances that fully justify what you have said."

"Yes, and so could I!" said George Berkeley; "several who, I feel, might have been saved by early marriage from being what they now are—the mere butterflies of society." And then he added, and from the sound of his voice Lucy almost fancied that he was turning more expressly to her, and that for moments his eyes must have been upon her, "And this," he said, "is only one view of the case; there is another, though less prejudicial perhaps to the character, more trying to the feelings. Let him love with all the devotion and unselfishness of which a man's nature is capable—let him dare to hope that the woman whom he loves might perhaps be won to care for him"—there was a slight hesitation, Lucy thought, in his voice, as he said this—"might perhaps be won, if he had liberty to urge his suit; still he is doomed to silence, he is bound in honour not to tie her down to any engagement, not to wound her delicacy by asking for an avowal of her love whilst he is unable to ask her to be his wife, whilst he is—just what I am, too poor to marry!"

George Berkeley stopped.

Mrs. Henry Wilton said, "I wish Lord Englefield could have heard you! I agree so heartily with you, that I must own I have often longed to preach to papas and mammas. Not you, dear granny," she said, laying her hand affectionately on old Mrs. Wilton's arm, " but to worldly papas and mammas, who have held forth to their sons, in my hearing, on the prudence of delay, and the merit of heiress hunting. And, on the other side," she added, laughing, "I should like to preach to such men as Lord Englefield or Lord Crawford, who will not marry."

" Perhaps they may have been unlucky in their attachments, though, my dear," said old Mrs. Wilton. " What do you hear of this, Mr. Berkeley?" she said, looking up at him from her spectacles. " You live in London society, so you know more about these things."

Mr. Berkeley coloured a little, then smiled rather sarcastically, and said, " I think Lord Englefield has better taste than Lord Crawford, but I cannot determine whether he is most to be pitied or despised;" and a glance at Lucy, as he said this very pointedly, brought such painful blushes on her cheeks, and made her work away so diligently at the shadows in her drawing, that they became quite black.

"Oh, Miss Crofton! pray don't touch that any more!" said Mrs. Henry Wilton. "I have been watching your pretty sketch, hoping I should get it when it was done; but you are shading too violently."

George Berkeley pushed his chair from the table. "Are we to have no music, Mrs. Wilton?" he said.

"Oh, dear yes! do have some. I was just wishing for it," said old Mrs. Wilton.

"Mary, my dear"—to Mrs. Henry—"will you play to us; and I hope we shall have some singing when Miss Crofton has finished her drawing."

George Berkeley looked quickly up at Lucy, and as she raised her head to answer Mrs. Wilton, she could not escape his eye.

"Can I help you to find your songs?" he said; and he persisted in looking at her for an answer.

"Oh, thank you!" she said, hastily; "they are all on the piano-forte."

"Then you need not leave your drawing," he said, "till Mrs. Henry Wilton has finished playing;" and he drew a chair near to hers. He was determined not to let her confusion subside.

"You did not enter into our discussion," he said, still looking at her. "You thought, perhaps, I spoke too warmly. And yet," he added, with still more emphasis, " I did not speak half as warmly as I felt. You are angry, perhaps," he said; "angry that we poor younger sons should dare to feel."

Lucy looked up one instant, whilst her cheek brightly flushed. " How can you be so unjust !" was all she said. She was too much agitated to say more. She moved her chair—she got up and joined Mrs. Henry Wilton at the piano. George Berkeley did not follow her. There was a hasty little pencil sketch that she had scribbled in the intervals of finishing the larger drawing; it was meant for one of the children, who had begged her to draw the boat, and the lake, and the mountain, and themselves. After the music was over, Lucy returned to put by her portfolio. Mr. Berkeley was again near her.

"You have made this little sketch of our boating party," he said, taking up the drawing. " Though I may not ask what others dare to do"—he hesitated a minute—" what the wealthy may dare to ask," was added in a lower voice, looking earnestly at her—" you will not refuse me the possession of this remembrance? I may be very long absent. This little sketch will have a value for me—an inestimable value ! Will you grant me this—as yet—all that I dare ask?" and Lucy could give no answer but one short, quick look, at his pleading face; but she did not refuse the drawing.

Others came up. There was a general talk about a delightful plan for the next day; and after the usual "good-nights," Lucy escaped *with* her happiness to her own room. And yet those were sad words which were resting on her ears— "absent"—"long absent"—"too poor to marry"— but what were they if George Berkeley really loved her?

CHAPTER XX.

The next day was as beautiful as the children could desire. The last day's party—the last day's excursion across the lake took place.

"I shall sit by you—close up!" said little Charlie Wilton, to Lucy.

"And I shall sit just close up on the other side!" said Mary Wilton; "and you will sing to us—just once—that little, little song."

The day was very delightful, and Lucy was happy; but sometimes, perhaps, she would have been content if the children had not clung quite so constantly around her. Mr. Berkeley once or twice drew near, and began to talk—just began to speak gravely and sadly—and then the children rushed up to bring a bunch of flowers, or to beg her to come and look at the most darling little stream, or to get Mr. Berkeley just to help them to climb one very steep rock, where there was a

VOL. I. I

hole that must be the den of one of those dragons he had told them about. And this was indeed Lucy's last day at Fernmere—her last day in George Berkeley's society for very long—how long she dare not think!

And the evening was coming on, and they must all go home. The three children, and grandpapa, and grandmamma, were already in the boat.

"What say you to walking home round the lake?" said George Berkeley. "It is a short cut and a beautiful path," appealing to Mrs. Henry Wilton and Lucy, who were still on shore. "You know how soon you get to your own wood walk," he said, addressing Mrs. Henry Wilton.

"Oh, let us walk!" she said, "if Miss Crofton will not be tired," turning to Lucy.

Lucy scarcely dared to own how much she preferred the walk with George Berkeley and Mrs. Henry Wilton, in that calm evening, to the boat, with the children clustering round her. But she only said quietly that she should like it.

"Let us set off, then," said Mrs. Henry Wilton, and she called to the party in the boat to say that they were going to walk home.

There was a shout of disapproval from the children, and a call for "dear Miss Crofton!" but Lucy was not obliged to attend to it, and

George Berkeley would not listen, and they set off.

The conversation was chiefly between Mrs. Henry Wilton and him, and yet, though they talked together, Lucy felt that all Mr. Berkeley said was chiefly for her. Lord Englefield was again brought on the *tapis*.

" He is a man I cannot fancy in love," said Mrs. Henry Wilton, laughing. " I never saw him the least approaching that way, but I think he need not fear a repulse if he tried his chance."

" I have seen him in love," said George Berkeley, " and I have seen him repulsed;" and Lucy knew that he was looking at her.

"Indeed!" said Mrs. Wilton. " I honour the young lady who repulsed him !"

" So do I," was George Berkely's short, pointed reply.

" But will he persevere, or did the young lady give him a decided rejection?" said Mrs. Wilton.

George Berkeley hesitated a moment, then said, "This remains to be proved. I have told you all I know."

" Look at that streak of light !" said Mrs. Wilton. " How beautiful it is! I love this point of view, and I am so glad you made us walk."

Lucy could have said, "So am I!" but she prudently kept the words to herself.

They soon came to the entrance of the grounds, nearly a mile from the house. Whether out of good-nature, or out of unconsciousness, I cannot tell, but Mrs. Henry Wilton said to Lucy—

"Perhaps you will not mind going on without me, for there is a poor woman in this cottage I am anxious to visit, and I shall just have time to see her, as no one will be in a hurry to go in on this lovely evening. You can walk gently, and Mr. Berkeley, I know, can show you the way."

Lucy could not object, and she and George Berkeley proceeded alone. They talked for a time very quietly and rationally, on the enjoyment of scenery such as this, and on the effect on the mind of living amongst it; but by degrees Mr. Berkeley dropped the general tone—he spoke of his own feelings, and of Lucy's.

"Let us stop here a moment," he said; "just here, where we can see the lake, and the island, and the boat. I want to get the scene by heart, that I may have it constantly before me when I am away. This scene—just as I see it now—just as I have seen it often in this happy year and the last! when you were with me," was added in a low voice. "Will you, too, remember it? Will you, too, think of it sometimes, when you are away?" he asked.

Lucy did not, could not speak at first. "I shall be very sorry to leave Fernmere," was all she could utter.

"You *are* sorry to leave then? You feel some regret?" George Berkeley said, quickly; and then added, more quietly, "You have been happy here, Miss Crofton," he said, "you like the people, and the scenery, and the sort of gipsey life?— Yes; these are questions I may safely ask! may I not?"

Lucy was afraid of betraying too much of her feelings—the feelings that were just then almost overpowering her—so she answered rather coldly, that she had been very happy at Fernmere.

George Berkeley looked hurt. "That is a civil assent!" he said, drawing back a little. "You would say equally that you had been very happy at Digby Manor, or at Hillesden, or at home! I see exactly what you feel! Whilst to me these weeks at Fernmere have been different from any other I ever spent in my life, they have been to you a mere passing pleasure."

Lucy turned quickly towards him—"I shall never forget Fernmere!" was said before she had the power to stop herself.

George Berkeley did not speak for a few minutes; then he said in a hurried, agitated manner, "You promise not to forget it! You promise, then?" and he looked eagerly at her. But he drew back; his tone changed, as if with a violent effort over himself, and he added, "I feel sure that you would never forget your friends."

There was a silence. George Berkeley walked quietly at her side, and when he began to speak again it was in a grave, composed tone. It was more like that of an affectionate friend, less like that of a lover, and it lessened Lucy's happy, yet half painful agitation.

"It is difficult," he said, "to speak or to think without pain of a separation, after having passed many happy weeks with those whom we value. I may have to go abroad. I do not know when we may meet again! The Wiltons are very kind friends! It has been a very happy time here— very happy!" he repeated.

Lucy was glad that her face could scarcely be seen, in the growing twilight. She tried to speak steadily, but her voice trembled a little as she said, "I think no one could help being happy with the Wiltons."

"No," George Berkeley said; "but for the pain of parting, this time would be stamped on my mind as the brightest in my life; but to think that this is our last evening together! I shall perhaps hear of you. You will sometimes be at Digby Manor. I saw you first there; do you remember?" he asked. "I shall like to fancy that I am not quite forgotten when you are sitting again with Miss Spencer in that dear, comfortable library. Next to Fernmere, that is the room I now love best in the world! Yesterday you let me hear that German song again I first heard there! I have a peculiar love for that song—a selfish, jealous affection for it! Would you make a sacrifice for me, and humour my folly and presumption by giving me a promise never to sing it to any one till we meet again? Am I too presumptuous?" he added, eagerly.

"Oh!" said Lucy, before she was aware what she had uttered, "I could never bear to sing it when you were away."

George Berkeley caught at the words. "Miss Crofton!" he began, passionately, "Miss Crofton! you would miss me, then? You would feel it?" But he checked himself, and added, more quietly, "This is very kind." And now they drew near the house. "Oh! not yet!" he exclaimed. "We cannot go in yet! Remember, Miss Crofton, it is our last evening."

"I am afraid it is late," said Lucy.

"No, not at all," said George Berkeley, eagerly. "It is a sin to go in yet! You remember Mrs. Henry Wilton said we need not hurry! Indeed, it is very early. I don't believe any of the party are at home; and I have never seen you alone all day! You will take my arm, will you not?"

Lucy did not refuse, and they walked on, and they talked again, more calmly. George Berkeley spoke of his objects in life—of the hard headwork he had constantly filling up his time—his sense that this work was not *the* object in life, and yet that it ought to be done diligently and zealously.

"But there is a higher work," he said, "that you, and I, and all of us have equally to perform; my fears are that this work should be forgotten in the constant wear and tear of mind that business such as mine involves. It is difficult sometimes to look on to nobler and better aims, in the midst of the fatigue and stretch of attention required from us in our daily avocations. When we see the grandest intellects of men brought to bear on subjects of vital importance for good or for evil to our own generation—if not to future ones—when we are working under those whose decisions must affect the whole progress of social life—it is difficult not to consider all these great and stirring interests as of paramount importance—it is difficult to recollect at such times that life is given us but as a trial scene, for work indeed, and for using every talent to the utmost of our power, but where the dull, ignorant, prosy old woman may rank higher than the men of greatest intellect and mental vigour. But," he added, "these dangers are nothing new to me, and it has been my habitual struggle, though often, alas! a feeble and a failing one, to keep my mind and heart as free as I can from their evil influence. But now," he added, "there is a new trial—a new difficulty."

Lucy turned quickly to look in his face and ask what this was.

"Yes," he added, looking at her, "a new trial, and yet so sweet, so precious in some of its phases, that I cannot, I would not for worlds lose its sweetness or its preciousness, in spite of all the pain and sorrow it brings me—it may bring to me! To know that after this evening I must leave you!—that all these delicious hours will be things of remembrance alone!—that I may meet with such difficulties as to prolong my absence! But you will not doubt me," he said. "If I am long absent, you will believe that duty alone keeps me away?" He paused.

Lucy felt her arm slightly pressed.

"Miss Crofton!" he said, in a lower and more tender voice, "will you believe in me—trust in me; will you remember me—as a friend?" was added, "you will not refuse to think of me as a friend, however long I may be separated from you?"

Lucy's faint reply was hardly audible, but George Berkeley was satisfied as long as that little trembling arm rested so lovingly on his. There were but few more words uttered; they were not needed. They lingered a little longer to gaze together on the calm sky, and then they must tear themselves away. They must go in and seem careless and indifferent, and mix again among the cheerful party in the lighted rooms and talk on the various topics of the day, as if these, the most sweet and blissful moments of their existence had had no reality.

CHAPTER XXI.

It was the end of October. It had been a very mild season, and the dahlias and the geraniums in the parsonage garden at Hulse were manfully fighting against the first approaches of frost, and Mrs. Walter was beginning, for the hundredth time, to bewail her singular ill luck in having Hulse House inhabited by an ungentlemanlike atheistical madman, whose hot house might have supplied her with a new stock of plants for next year, had he been a sane and orthodox person, when the door was thrown wide open with peculiar *empressement* and dignity, and the servant, in a voice of half-suppressed awe and amazement, said—

"Mr. Colville, ma'am!" and in walked Mr. Colville himself.

Even Lucy started, and looked at their visitor in momentary surprise and curiosity; whilst Mrs.

Walter stared, bowed, and curtsied with all the flurry of vulgar amazement, as Mr. Colville uttered his first civil, gentle words.

"I must introduce myself, Mrs. Crofton, as I am sorry to find that your husband is not at home."

"Oh, yes! Mr. Crofton, he is—that is, he is not—I fear he is gone out! We are very happy, I am sure—Mr. Crofton has the pleasure—he told me—he tells me—a very pleasant house—Hulse House. I hope you find it comfortable?" Mrs. Walter stammered forth, whilst Arthur Colville, with a proud, calm air, stood condescending to listen.

"Pray sit down," she said at last, recovering a little of her composure, on finding Mr. Colville much like any other person, with neither wildness nor ferocity in his eyes. "Pray sit down," and Mr. Colville accepted the offered chair.

In spite of the calm, half haughty civility of his manner, it appeared to Lucy that he was agitated and almost overcome by this first break to his entire seclusion from society, and yet his apparent calmness and his slightly sarcastic tone, when he replied to Mrs. Walter's attempts at conversation, almost belied the idea that he could feel anything like emotion in the mere presence of those he seemed to despise. He did not look at Lucy, and she hoped to escape his observation entirely, when, to her dismay, Mrs. Walter said—

"Mr. Colville, pray allow me to introduce Miss Crofton, Mr. Crofton's sister."

Lucy half rose; Mr. Colville stood up and bowed low, but he said not a word; and, as he sat down again, he resumed the very uninteresting conversation with Mrs. Crofton. At last, Mrs. Crofton's courage rose, and Lucy blushed painfully for Mr. Colville's sake as well as their own, as Mrs. Walter said, very benignly—

"You have lived quite a solitary life of late, Mr. Colville; but I hope you will not always deprive us of the pleasure of your company. We do not give dinner parties in our small house, but we should feel much flattered if you would dine here quietly some day."

Mr. Colville stooped down as Mrs. Walter began her sentence, probably to conceal the indignant flush which mounted to his temples as she spoke; and then, with almost a stern manner, he said, very coldly, but with studied civility—

"I thank you, Mrs. Crofton, but I never leave home; I lead a solitary life, as you say, and I have no intention of breaking a resolution which was not rashly formed." He drew himself up and coloured, as if his very pride added to his embarrassment, as he said, "Excuse me when I explain that my visit to-day is not the mere formal visit of one country neighbour to another. Mr. Crofton benevolently acceded to my request, when I ventured to send for him." And then he smiled rather ironically, as he said, " I have made rules for myself! I am under a sort of self-imposed vow, if you like to call it so, and my vow forbids me from seeing any one but the clergyman of my parish and his family. I should be glad of the privilege of coming here occasionally, if you could kindly make it possible for me to do so, by securing to me the certainty of meeting no one but yourselves when I call upon you."

Mrs. Walter was quite overcome! "Oh! certainly! certainly!" she said. "Indeed, I feel much flattered· by your kindness in making an exception in our favour."

She would have been very angry with any other person who had dared to view her merely as the clergyman's wife, but something in Mr. Colville's manner awed, whilst it captivated her, and she was ready to say all and more than all the civil things that were required from her.

Mr. Colville soon took leave, and when he was gone, Mrs. Walter exclaimed—

"I never saw a more gentlemanlike, agreeable
man! After the first moment, when I really
hardly knew which way to look or what to say, I
think I seldom spent a pleasanter half hour! My
dear Lucy! depend upon it, before a year is over,
he will be dining with us as comfortably as any-
body else; and with his wealth, and no doubt
very good connexions (for I never saw a more
distinguished looking person), there is no saying
what an advantage he might be to us! He
seemed much pleased with this house, and I
thought he spoke very kindly of Walter," and so
Mrs. Walter ran on till her husband came home,
and then she had the pleasure of revealing to him
the wonderful event that had occurred, and of
seeing him as much surprised and gratified as she
could desire. She was eager to go the round of
the parish and tell her neighbours everything that
had passed; but, to her vexation, Walter requested
her to say as little as possible about Mr. Colville,
excepting to their few very intimate friends, such
as old Miss Walcott (who, we must say, *en passant*,
stood high in Walter's esteem). Mr. Colville had,
as it were, confided himself to them; he had
come solely out of respect for Mr. Crofton's
clerical office, and he had bound them, therefore,
by every sentiment of honour, not to make these

interviews the subject of common gossip. Walter spoke so decidedly and seriously that Mrs. Walter had only to submit; but after a short fit of ill-humoured despondency, the charms of Mr. Colville's visit, with the permission to tell Miss Walcott all about it, restored her to more than composure.

CHAPTER XXII.

THE sunshine of Miss Walcott's cottage shed its influence on many different classes of minds. To Walter Crofton, half an hour at Woodbine Cottage was the pleasant reward for a hard day's word in the parish, for he and the little lady were staunch friends.

The next time he visited her, after they had discussed politics, literature, and metaphysics, Miss Walcott launched forth about Mr. Colville.

" Your wife tells me he has been to see her, and that he is nothing short of Diogenes, Solomon, or Apollo, she can't exactly tell me which !" she said with a short, scornful laugh. " But what do you say to him, Walter Crofton?" and her sharp black eyes looked at him for an answer.

Walter told what had passed between them.

" Yes, yes !" said the little lady, " that will do. I see it all ! He is to be pitied ! He is a great dolt of a man for all that; shutting himself up, indeed! But there is metal in him, from what you say; though it seems to be mixed up with a good share of dross!" she added, with a little chuckle. "A fine young man, is he?" she asked.

"His countenance struck me particularly," said Walter.

"Yes—hum!—and that was all you noticed, no doubt! but your wife tells me that he is tall and handsome. So much the better! for he will be more anxious to come out and show himself, when he has sickened of his folly. Keep to him, Walter Crofton! He is a great dolt, and I say it again, but if he were but half witted, he would be worth saving! And to think of this great simpleton, who can read!—who can study Horace and quote Shakespeare!—going and hiding himself because he has had some smart slap in the face! Yes! he has popped himself into the furnace of affliction, and let him have enough of it! Let him boil well! It will do him good! But keep to him, Walter Crofton! Poor soul! poor soul!" she added, with a changed voice. "Quite alone! quite alone! he said, did he?" then changing back, with her short, sharp, bleat of a laugh; "and whose fault is that? When a man goes up in a balloon (and that is about as silly a bit of tom-foolery as I know), he does not go and cry because he is up in the air; and when I lock my door, I don't sit bellowing because I'm locked in! Trash! fudge! Not thirty, did you say? Poor youth! poor youth! A great lumbering brained lout! Stick to him, Walter Crofton! If you don't pull him out, I will! I'll be packed up and go to him, and shake my wig at him, cap and all! It makes one angry to think of it! Not thirty, and to shut himself up!"

When Walter Crofton was gone, the little lady still muttered to herself, "Not thirty! Poor youth! poor youth?" and in the sharp, black eyes there were two tears, very quickly wiped away when another visitor was announced.

Miss Walcott was seldom without visitors, for there was something so cheerful and sympathetic in the welcome at Woodbine Cottage, that if any were in trouble they came to be pitied, and if any were happy they came to be laughed with; and if Miss Walcott scolded or snubbed no one felt chafed by it.

And now the dullest of old maids arrived, but Miss Walcott was as brisk as ever in her welcome; and as the old maid had a long, prosy account to give of her own health and spirits, Miss Walcott only dashed in at times with her remarks, such as a "hum!" or a short laugh, or a "Bless you! take some rhubarb!" or "low spirited were you, yesterday evening, in the dusk? Why did not you come to me, you old simpleton? People are never low spirited with me!" "Afraid of troubling me? Nonsense! Stuff! How could you trouble me? What, you felt all in a palpitation, did you?" as the old woman enlarged on her ailments. "Just give my compliments to your Molly, and tell her when you are all palpitating next time, to wrap you up and send you off to me. Palpitation! nobody ever palpitates when they come here!" and the old lady went away smiling and laughing, and promising to give Miss Walcott's message to Molly, and she had no more palpitations for some days.

It is a pity there are not more Woodbine Cottages in the world! Little Miss Walcott was poor—she had lost all her near relations—a rheumatic fever, some years back, had made her a cripple—in earlier days a long engagement to a good and clever but poor man had been ended by his death. Miss Walcott could not, therefore, be called a prosperous person, but though we, some of us, are rich, and some of us have affectionate relations, and some of us marry our early loves, and some of us are in vigorous health, we do not all of us catch the sun as Miss Walcott does in her Woodbine Cottage!

"I don't think London agrees with you," said Mrs. Walter to Edward Crofton, as he was wishing her good-bye, after a short visit to the parsonage.

"Why not?" said Edward, shortly; "women never understand that men must work. If it did not agree with me (which it does) I must live there all the same."

"No," said Mrs. Walter; "you could come oftener to visit poor Walter, who never grumbles at your absence, and yet of course he feels it very much. I know you could come here oftener if you wished it, and I am sure London disagrees with you, whatever you may say to the contrary, for you are as pale and thin as a shadow, and Lucy could tell you so, only she never likes agreeing with anything I say."

"Well," said Edward, "I will leave you and Lucy to settle that point, and now I must be off, or I shall lose the coach, so good-bye;" and Mrs. Walter, as usual, was quieted down by Edward's sturdy indifference to her unreasonable bits of ill-temper, and shook his hand heartily, and after an affectionate kiss to Lucy he was gone.

Lucy's eyes were rather red with tears, when Barker Preston was ushered in soon afterwards. He saw it, and he was as awkwardly gentle as his nature allowed. He said he liked to see a woman feel a thing, and love for a brother was the very thing he meant. It really pleased him excessively; that is, Miss Crofton would understand—it made him very miserable! He would rather, at any time, lose a good day's hunting! In short, she would understand exactly what he meant. He, himself, could be unhappy! yes, indeed he could; and no one knew why! He could assure her, no one in the least knew why! and that was the very reason why he was so sorry for her!"

And Lucy smiled, and thanked him for his sympathy, as she said, "I am, indeed, very sorry to part with Edward."

"And so, Mrs. Crofton," said Barker Preston, "you have had a visit from Mr. Colville!"

"Yes," said Mrs. Walter, "yes, indeed! we have had a very interesting visit, and I would tell you all about it, but that we feel ourselves bound to silence. Mr. Colville has treated us exactly like friends, and to show you what peculiarly confidential circumstances we are placed in, even now, should he repeat his visit, I should be obliged to send you away."

" Send me away !" exclaimed Barker Preston, laughing heartily. " You might send me, Mrs. Crofton, but should I go, that's all !"

Mrs. Crofton angrily assured him that he certainly must. " This is no joking matter, Mr. Preston," she said.

" No more it is !" said Barker Preston, more gravely, " and to tell you the truth, I pity the poor fellow heartily ; so let's talk no more about it ! I am only glad he has been to see you. I am sure you will do him good, Miss Crofton."

CHAPTER XXIII.

THE geraniums and dahlias had become blackened with the frost, and the falling leaves of the forest trees had been finally swept away, and the snow had more than once covered the ground; the snowdrop had flowered and faded, and the primrose had reappeared with all its refreshing recollections before Mr. Colville repeated his visit to the parsonage.

Mrs. Walter Crofton's cheerful predictions upon their first acquaintance had not been realised. How that winter wore on to him in his still unbroken loneliness I will not try to relate.

When Lucy saw him again she could have shuddered as she observed the increased sternness and melancholy of his expression, and Walter Crofton thought of him with deep pain now that the terrible suspicion had dawned upon him that Mr. Colville was almost an unbeliever. Their first day's discussion on theological subjects had led to several others, and Walter saw that Mr. Colville's mind was gradually darkening under the influence of his lonely, profitless existence.

The only cheerful prospect throughout the wide domain of Hulse House was the throng of labourers working at the various improvements and alterations on the property. These alterations had been set on foot by Mr. Colville, for the purpose of giving employment to the poor; but even here the shadow of eccentricity fell rather unpleasantly. Mr. Colville's whimsical exercise of charity in hiring any vagrant who chose to ask for a day's work was not a little trying to the feelings of his steward and gardener, who, not having secluded themselves from the world, had still an interest in good crops and neat work.

As the steward was walking round the park one day, after a despairing glance at the reposing attitudes of several of Mr. Colville's mendicant labourers, his temper was tried by a fresh application. A poor woman came up to the fence and begged for employment in the garden.

"My good woman......" the steward began, in rather an imperious tone, but at this instant Mr. Colville came near.

VOL. I. K

"What is this, Jackson?" he called out rather sharply.

"A poor woman, sir, wants work in the garden," was the reply, in an altered tone.

"Let her be employed, then," said Mr. Colville.

"But, sir, I doubt if she can do much good!" in a deprecating tone.

Mr. Colville's brow lowered. "Let her be employed," he said, in a decided manner, and he rode away; whilst the steward, inwardly murmuring at his master's caprice, returned to speak to the woman whom he had left outside the park fence. She had disappeared! He called and called, but there was no answer! At last he went through the gate, and there he saw her resting on the ground and weeping bitterly. The steward was kind-hearted although surly in manner.

"Come, come, my good woman!" he called out, "cheer up! You are to be employed. So, come along! and cheer up, I say!"

The woman hastily rose, as the steward addressed her, and wiping her eyes with her apron, she thanked him in her own rude way, and followed him to the pleasure grounds, where he gave her in charge to one of the under gardeners, with a few private words of information as to her admission. The woman's face was much concealed by a red handkerchief, and a coarse and not very clean cap which came far over it. She was slightly lame, and her large, clumsy, men's boots gave her an awkward shuffling gait. As she began her task of hoeing up weeds, the gardener's eye occasionally glanced at her from a little distance.

"No great hand at work, I see plainly enough!" he said to another of the garden men; "but I suppose that rich gentlefolks must be indulged in all their whims!"

For two days the woman continued her employment, without any very evident increase of knowledge on the subject of weeds, but with much more on that of "the squire," about whom she and the other weeding women gossipped a great deal. The new comer seemed determined not to be outdone by her companions in their wonderful stories about Mr. Colville, and she often made them laugh heartily at the amusing tales she told of strange, eccentric beings she pretended to have met with in her life. As she talked and laughed with her companions no one could have thought her unhappy, and yet, as she walked home alone to the cottage where she lodged, she was often in tears. Whether her tears were caused by distress of mind, or by mere weariness of body it was difficult to divine. She certainly did not trouble herself in any very active warfare against the weeds which had been handed over to her jurisdiction, and the gardener did not dare to find fault, for fear of his master's displeasure.

"Very trying to the gardener! who evidently was an honest, hard-working man," broke in my sister Martha. "Ten to one if the woman did not destroy some of his best plants with her clumsy weeding."

"Ah! poor thing!" said Jane, "that would be a pity! But I dare say she meant well, and I am sure she had some great trouble, in spite of her amusing tales!"

"Mr. Colville, at any rate, thought she had the trouble of poverty," I continued; "and as he caught a distant sight of her gray cloak when he at length resolved to ride to the parsonage he dwelt with much pleasure on the thought of his own benevolence."

Mr. Colville set out by a circuitous route, as if to brace himself by brisk exercise for the effort of the visit to the Croftons. After a gallop, he let his horse walk gently along, and as his pace slackened, his thoughts became active.

Many scenes in his past life presented themselves to his memory; the voices of his former companions—the very jests that had been common between them, came flickering across his brain like ghosts of themselves. While the illusion lasted it was a soothing one; but as it gradually faded away, and the harsh, cold outline of the present stood forth again, the contrast to these dream-like images made it appear more hard and painful than ever. The idea of going to the parsonage became unbearable. He turned his horse's head, and was soon riding back to the dungeon from which he had planned a temporary escape.

As he entered his own grounds at one of the lodges, the poor woman of whom I have just spoken was walking slowly home from her work. A turn in the road brought her in view of Mr. Colville. She stopped and curtsied.

Mr. Colville had at all times a nervous dread of being seen: his mind at this moment was but little in a state for interruption. It seemed as if his most secret communings had been impertinently intruded upon. Grief turned to passion: fixing his eyes in sudden anger upon the woman, he muttered an oath, and spurring his horse, he galloped forwards, and was quickly out of sight.

The woman stood motionless, her eyes following the rider as long as she could see him, and when he at last disappeared in the distance, she began to walk home slowly and sadly, almost as if in pain, and sobbing at times as if her heart would break.

Week passed after week, and she never reappeared in the garden at Hulse. As her wages were unpaid, the gardener, at length, sent to inquire about her at the cottage where he was told that she had lodged. He found that she had left it for some time and no one could give any information of her movements.

CHAPTER XXIV.

WE must remember that Mr. Colville's unfortunate rencontre with the poor weeding-woman was entirely unknown to Mrs. Walter Crofton, who, about this time, had arrived at a settled conviction that Mr. Colville was neither a lunatic nor an atheist, but, on the contrary, that he was exactly the person to suit Lucy as a husband. He had certainly not yet shown any preference for her, but everything had a beginning and an ending (excepting dust, of which there was no end). Mr. Colville was rich and good-looking—Hulse House was large and commodious. It was in their immediate neighbourhood; as a young wife, Lucy would often want her advice; between the manor house and the parsonage there would be a constant interchange of luxuries and of good counsel. What could be more desirable! And when, at last the long-wished-for words sounded in her ears—

"Mr. Colville, ma'am, wishes to know if you are alone?" she answered with animation, "Yes, yes! show him in! and remember the order, to admit no one whilst Mr. Colville is with us, James.

"Lucy, my dear, place that chair a little more comfortably near your drawing-table—there—so;" and Mr. Colville walked in.

But if Mrs. Walter thought that he would take any interest in Lucy's drawing, she was mistaken. His cheerless glance betrayed a careless contempt for everything that was going on. Mrs. Walter's attempts to speak of Lucy's singing, or to display her drawings, or to touch upon the gossip of the neighbourhood, or the topics of the day, were met by him, as usual, with such chilling indifference, that even she could not persevere in forcing them on his notice. Under these circumstances, to a mind such as hers, conversation was almost impossible; and as she was very willing to leave him alone with Lucy, after having gone through the usual remarks on the state of the roads, the quantity of rain on Monday, and of wind on Tuesday, she said,

"Perhaps you will excuse me, Mr. Colville, for a few minutes, as some poor people are waiting to see me?"

Mr. Colville bowed, said a few civil words, and Mrs. Walter left the room.

Lucy felt a little shy at being left alone with their strange, abstracted visitor, but she exerted herself to break the silence which ensued, as Mrs. Walter quitted them. She had a group of flowers before her, which she was trying to sketch.

"I do not wonder at the universal love of flowers," she said. "They seem more inimitable and more beautiful every moment one watches them!"

"They have even outlived the praises of the would-be poets," said Mr. Colville, drily.

"They would outlive anything that was wanting in grace or beauty," said Lucy, and she looked up at Mr. Colville and smiled, and for the first time she met his eye.

Habitual as it is to us to talk with others, to catch their meaning from the expression in their faces, we can hardly conceive what it must be to live without this natural interchange of ideas. For many years Mr. Colville had purposely done so— he had purposely kept aloof from every social interest or sympathy—and all at once a slight and scarcely tangible incident—merely the chance of his eye resting on Lucy Crofton's face as she looked up at him and smiled—seemed, as it were, to knock at his heart, touching every chord of feeling, awakening every dormant emotion; he felt that he was again one amongst others, one who could be sympathised with, one who could sympathise with others!

A smile of great sweetness lighted up his countenance, and then, strange as it was, even a tear glistened in his eye! He shaded his face for an instant, and whole years of his life seemed condensed into that one small point of time! It is almost impossible to describe or define the vehemence of his emotion. It was suddenly excited, and as suddenly dispelled; for before he again looked up, before Lucy was in the least aware of what had been passing in his mind, his softer feelings were chilled down, the tumultuous current of reviving sympathies and affections so curiously unloosed was frozen back into rigidity, and his first words were uttered in his usual, half-ironical tone.

Mrs. Walter returned to the drawing-room; a few uninteresting remarks were all that followed. Mr. Colville expressed a hope that Mr. Crofton would kindly come over to Hulse House, and then he left them.

"Perhaps a proposal for Lucy!" Mrs. Walter thought, with delightful excitement, as she returned with increased elasticity to the mysteries of cross stitch.

"Well, Mr. Crofton?" said she, eagerly, to Walter, as he entered the room next day, after his visit to Mr. Colville; "well?"

"Well, my dear!" Walter said; "what is the matter?"

"Oh! nothing the matter," was the desponding reply; "only I wished to know what Mr. Colville wanted you for."

"A question in theology," said Walter, "which has been often raised and as often settled."

"Theology, indeed!" said Mrs. Crofton, angrily; "I should have thought you might have found something better to talk about than that!"

CHAPTER XXV.

It is towards the end of April. It had been a gay, pretty morning, succeeded by a soft and sunny afternoon; and as Lucy Crofton gently sauntered through the pleasure-grounds at the parsonage, she felt very happy—she scarcely knew why, except that there was something inspiring in the delicious air, and the beauty of every object around her. She sat down to look at the primroses on the banks of the stream, and to watch the stream itself as it went bubbling and sparkling on over its gray stones, and by degrees she forgo the flowers, and the stream, and the picturesque alders, and she thought only of her own happy love, and on this beautiful, cheerful day, doubt and fear gave place to hope, and she let herself wander into the future, and imagine what George Berkeley's words would be when they met, and how she could dare to tell him that she loved him!

She thought of the great joy of being beloved by one like him. She thought of his goodness even more than of his brilliant talents, or his personal attractions, or his inimitable conversational powers. These qualities were public, they were for all; but for her alone had been the confidential outpourings of mind and heart—the grave discussions on higher matters than mere worldly interests; and on these she pondered with sweet and tender recollection. Then she dwelt in thought on the singular justness and integrity of his character—his cheerful, animating view of life as a field for active virtues, active struggles against evil, active preparation for a future world, and grateful, lively enjoyment of all God's wonderful blessings here. Yes, this was her hero! this was the George Berkeley whom she loved, and who loved her!

In those times posts did not come in at every hour of the day as they do at present, and on this afternoon the letters were late. But Lucy fancied there might be one that would bring some pleasant tidings; for it was impossible not to have hope infused into the mind on such a cheerful day as this. And when Lucy went in, there really was a letter for her; but she did not know the handwriting or the post-mark, and for a minute or two the day seemed as if a cloud had come over it.

Lucy must go upstairs to take off her bonnet, and get ready for dinner, for the dressing-bell had just rung; so she carried her letter upstairs.

"Still," she thought, "to-morrow may bring another letter. I know he will try to meet me soon!" and the sun seemed to shine forth again—and indeed it did shine gaily into her room.

She sat down when she had taken off her bonnet and shawl, and then she took up the disappointing letter, and she opened it; and then Lucy—poor Lucy!—the sun shone no more for her on that day, nor for many, many days, to come! Still it had been a happy morning, and it is something in our lives to have experienced some such hours of enjoyment. Lucy saw that the handwriting was strange to her. She did not receive many letters, and the formal "Madam" at the beginning startled her—it somehow prepared her for the pain that followed—and her flushed cheek, her fast, thick breathing, her trembling hand as she read, left no doubt of the pain that letter caused.

It was as follows:

"Madam—I feel some difficulty in addressing you, and were I less certain of my right to do so, I should offer apologies and excuses which would sound more civil, but would only be less honest.

I will therefore state at once why I write, and what it is that I desire from you. My son George has confided to me his attachment, and he has asked my consent to offer himself to you. I do not know from him how far you have encouraged his addresses, or what chance he has of your acceptance if he asks you to become his wife. On this point I wish for no further information. I have been used to obedience from my children—I require it, I exact it—but I am proud to say, I depend still more on their love than on their duty. I have not brought up ungrateful children—my wishes are their law.

"I will not dally with words of compliment, but say at once that there are circumstances which make me strongly repugnant to the idea of my son's marriage with yourself—but on which I need not dilate: without money on your side it would, indeed, be *impossible* he should marry you. When he first told me of his attachment, he told me also that although he had openly shown his love for you, and he believed you to be fully aware of it, he had carefully refrained from involving you in a declaration of your own feelings for him until he had gained my consent to address you. This, then, was the time to stop the progress of so rash and inconsiderate an attachment. I forcibly pointed out to him the evils attending it; I urged him to see you no more. He told me his affections were given, and absence could not change his feelings towards you, nor would it consist with his honour to leave you for ever without farther explanation. He would not listen to my advice; I was obliged to insist. His first forgetfulness of the respect and obedience due to his mother was on this occasion—but I conquered. He promised to go abroad, without seeing you again, or writing to you. This was the most I could draw from him, and I, in my turn, was obliged to promise that if, at the end of a year, his feelings for you were unchanged, I would then allow him to declare himself. He left England in the autumn, for a year's absence.

"Now, Miss Crofton, I come to the point on which it is necessary I should appeal to you. After my son's departure, agitation of mind brought on a severe nervous illness. In the midst of it a serious calamity befel me. My eldest son had involved himself in speculations—I thank God with no dishonour! Good-natured weakness alone can attach to his conduct—dishonour rests on others! I need not particularise. We are placed in great difficulties for the present, unless some arrangements between my two sons can be carried out, which the marriage of George with yourself would render impossible, thus adding another tangible objection to the many very strong ones I already possessed against his engagement.

"Madam, it is needless, and too degrading and painful to me to lay before you these most private family concerns. I am old—I am worn down by much care. I have spent the energies of a long life in watching over the interests of my sons; towards the close of it, by the unlucky attachment of one of these sons, my tenderest feelings are deeply wounded; by the inadvertence of another, I find myself suddenly under the danger of losing all that long habit has made necessary to my existence. I have, it may be, strong prejudices; it is too late to eradicate them! My life must go with the attempt to tear them up. My health and my nerves have sunk under this last shock. Life and reason hang by a thread. It is in your power to cut that thread, as it is also in your power to restore to me the small remains of health and peace of mind of which my advanced age and shattered frame are capable. I ask you to make a noble sacrifice, and, believe me, madam, you will have your reward. There are blessings from the aged which outweigh golden years of joy. These will be yours, if you resign my son. I ask you, then, to promise that if, at the end of the allotted year, my son George should ask you to become his wife, you will unconditionally reject his addresses, without betraying the secret of my interference, and that you will never at any future time engage yourself to him without my consent. I wait anxiously, breathlessly for your answer. Take three days to consider it. Remember what it is you do, if you refuse my request, and may the blessing of that God who has given the unchangeable law—'Honour thy father and thy mother' *with a promise*, so rest on you if you now sever not parent and child.

"FRANCES BERKELEY."

In the same cover was enclosed another letter. Almost without taking breath Lucy began to read it; her eyes straining, her hand pressed tightly to her forehead, as if to enable her to take in the full amount of pain of what she had still to learn. This second letter was from the medical man who was attending Mrs. Berkeley.

We will simply state its purport in our own words. Mrs. Berkeley had told the writer that in the letter addressed to Miss Crofton, which she had begged him to forward, there was a request, the refusal of which she felt certain would be fatal to her. He said that Mrs. Berkeley had shown the greatest agitation in speaking of it; Dr. H—— thought it right, therefore, though perfectly ignorant of the nature of the request, to add a few words of caution, unknown to his patient. Mrs. Berkeley, he said, was just recovering from a short but severe illness, which had fallen on the nerves, and he had very little doubt that if anything happened strongly to agitate her at this crisis her reason would at once give way. If, therefore, Miss Crofton could reasonably grant the request, on which so much depended, he need hardly recommend her to do so. The letter was kindly and sensibly written—it was only too horribly matter of fact and true.

There are struggles in the heart which cannot be told in words—sudden anguish coming upon unusual joy—sudden hopelessness upon unusual hopefulness. The sparkling brook, the gray stones, the peaceful primrose roots nestling in the bank, the picturesque alder trees, the blithe warbling birds, the delicious sensation of sun and air and sweet scents and sounds, the soft, happy musings, the joyful, grateful aspirations, half prayer half praise, that were with Lucy Crofton but half an hour back, as she sat by the running stream, were now to her as far away—as impossible to realise—as any romance of fairy land; there was such a gulf of misery between herself and those happy moments.

And yet the full amount of her sorrow had not made itself known to her! its very suddenness and novelty gave a slight relief, imparting a certain doubt and excitement. Even anxiety as to the common concerns of the day had its use in warding off the first brunt of misfortune. How to conceal her distress, how to appear at dinner, were questions so needful and so agitating that she was obliged to attend to them. She locked her door, and when the expected knock came, with the question, "Are you ready for me, ma'am?" from Mrs. Walter's maid, Lucy was able to say, "Presently, Wilson," and then to sink back, relieved for the moment, but alive to the necessity of some effort either to go down to dinner, or to make some excuse for not doing so.

The first idea was that she must go down as usual, and she started up to begin changing her dress, but sudden dizzy faintness showed her that this was impossible; then came the dread of her sister-in-law's sharp, hard questioning voice if she sent a message to say that she was ill. But the dinner bell was just beginning; she hastily unlocked the door, threw herself on the sofa, muffled up her face in a shawl, and when Wilson came, she begged her to tell her brother and sister that she had a bad headache and thought it better not to come down.

Wilson withdrew, and presently came a message to beg her to keep quiet, and that no doubt she would soon be better; and Wilson, making her promise to ring for some tea the moment she wanted it, left her to the "nice little sleep" she was sure would quite cure her. "And so I will tell my mistress not to disturb you," were her comforting last words, and Lucy was left alone.

CHAPTER XXVI.

When secure from intrusion Lucy drew forth the two letters, and again went through every word. Even then she could not read the strong expressions of George Berkeley's love for her, which his mother's letter conveyed, without a thrill of joy! and she took a deep breath, and then there was a glow of indignation at her heart as she thought— " Proud, worldly woman! why should I sacrifice his happiness and my own to her selfish caprice?" and for awhile, as she read on, she steeled herself against any feelings of pity. But then came the words that pleaded for consideration—it was George Berkeley's mother who wrote—" worn down with much care." " Life and reason hang by a thread!" Could she cut the thread by which " life and reason were held?" Could she kill George Berkeley's mother by her obstinate refusal? If Lucy could dare to brave Mrs. Berkeley's own words, she felt it was impossible to brave the warning that had been conveyed to her with such cruel kindness by the medical man. Her own happiness must be sacrificed rather than run the fearful risk his letter suggested to her. But then it was not her own happiness alone, it was his! it was George Berkeley's! Because his mother chose to deal falsely and treacherously by him, what right had she to do so?

Thus Lucy reasoned, and she tried to do so impartially; but how was it possible when her own heart pleaded so strenuously on one side alone?

There was a slight gleam of comfort as she thought that it would be justifiable to confide in Walter. But on farther consideration she rejected the idea, and settled that she must battle through her doubts in secret, as she could not ask for any advice without betraying a secret that was not simply her own. Real illness gave the excuse for solitary deliberation, which she so much needed. She was obliged to keep her room, with continued headache, and during that time her decision was made.

Lucy Crofton had the most gentle and yet the firmest of natures—the most tender and yet the bravest of spirits. She came to her decision with many tears and with earnest prayer, but having done so, she admitted to herself no farther hesitation in acting upon it. How often had Clara Wilton's clear voice, as she said, " And though my heart might break I never will marry him without her consent," and George Berkeley's enthusiastic reply, " I honour you!" sounded in her ears during those three days of deliberation! George Berkeley little knew how much his own words helped to decide Lucy against himself! Lucy's letter was written in a firm hand; it was sealed and sent. Its contents were as follows:—

" MADAM—After three days of solitary deliberation, I give the promise you require—that without your consent I will not accept an offer of marriage from Mr. George Berkeley, and that I will not betray to him the reason of my refusal.

" Whilst I give this promise, let me beg of you, madam, to remember what it is you exact. Your son has declared to you that his affections are fixed on me, and you plainly believe that my affections are bestowed on him in return. You ask of me, while youth gives promise of many years of existence, to cut off by my own act, not only my own happiness but, it may be, to bring much sorrow over the best years of your son's life

—a son, madam, whom you profess to love, and whom I now own, what I have never owned before to any human being, I love with all the devotion of which my heart is capable.

"Think, then, madam, what it is I have granted; and if, on calmer deliberation, you can cancel that which you exact from me, remember that to spare me any moment of that suffering, under which the mercy of God can alone support me, is a duty which I in return claim from you. And, madam, I also claim from you that you deal tenderly with my character in your son's eyes. If he must think me faithless and changeable, find for me some excuse consistent with the severity of your decision, but do not add to the pang of separation the misery of believing that I have been unjustly lowered in his esteem.

"And now, madam, that, out of respect for your character as *his* mother I have granted your request, I have to remind you of your own promise. Your blessing was offered if I acceded to your wishes; I need it. I need every prayer and every blessing that your heart and lips can frame, and when I say I forgive you for the blow you have given to a heart just daring to dwell on its dawning happiness, I feel justified in asking this from you. May God direct and guide you to what is right! and as you deal truly and honestly by your son and by me, so may God's blessing rest upon you in this life and the next!

"LUCY CROFTON."

Lucy had achieved her act of self-sacrifice. There was neither sympathy nor admiration to be gained by it. No one but the proud, selfish woman who had exacted it would ever be aware of what she had done, but Lucy's anxiety was to do what was right; whether she gained applause for her conduct or not was a matter of little importance to her.

CHAPTER XXVII.

The great strain on Lucy's mental powers, and the shock to her affections caused by Mrs. Berkeley's letter, brought on severe illness. Up to the moment when she was prostrated by it, her great anxiety had been how to appear before her brother and sister-in-law, and how to conceal her distress from them! The violent headaches which had kept her upstairs for these few days would, perhaps, no longer befriend her, and then it would be necessary for her to appear downstairs as if nothing unusual had happened. And must she carry this overpowering sense of misery with her, was her thought, and yet seem to be as usual? Must she be looked at and questioned, kindly and unkindly, and yet say nothing—shed not a tear? How would it be possible to bear it?

On the evening after she had written and sent the letter to Mrs. Berkeley, illness seemed creeping over her; before night she was in a high state of fever; and, as her pulse rose, the haunting terror of disclosing her secret amounted almost to delirium.

But she was now really ill; she was obliged to keep her bed, and the doctor was summoned. None but those whose minds have been thoroughly wearied out by some great anxiety can fully understand the relief it is when illness at length forces rest upon their exertions. Lucy felt it. She need not settle any longer how she should speak and look as she sat down stairs with Mrs. Walter and Walter—at least this perplexity and terror were removed ! But as this difficulty passed away another came more strongly in its place ! How could she help disclosing her secret if delirium came on ! and she knew—she guessed she had been delirious once or twice in that dreadful night.

And that letter ! that letter of George's mother's —that letter of the doctor's—how could they be concealed ? As the hours wore on she was constantly thinking of them. She knew she had locked them up, and yet now, in that dreadful night of fever, they seemed to lie spread out on her dressing table, the sun shining strongly upon every word, and Mrs. Walter peering at them and giving little short angry laughs as she read. And then, worse still, louder laughter came, for these very letters were spread out on the large drawing-room table at Digby Manor, and the whole party saw them, and Agnes Spencer was laughing very loudly and harshly, and her brother Edward laughed too; and when Lucy tried to snatch the letters away and hide them, he and Agnes held her hands so tightly whilst they laughed again and again, that she screamed out with pain, and then her eyes opened, and there sat Wilson, the maid, watching her anxiously, and there was one candle, and it was her own little room at home, and she dared to speak, and for a few minutes she knew that all the rest had been feverish sleep.

But then she remembered that part of it was not a dream, and again the letters grew and grew till they became of an enormous size, and again she struggled in vain to hide them; and then George Berkeley, with an angry look, held her back, and he changed into a cruel demon who was pushing her down a deep, dark abyss, and then she screamed; and again, the dimly lighted room revealed itself to her, and the doctor's face was there as well as Wilson's, and she tried to smile, for poor Wilson looked so anxious; but when she tried to smile a horrible discordant laugh and shriek seemed to come from her lips, and again she was in the drawing-room at Digby Manor, with grinning faces all around her, making a jest of her grief, and her heart was cold, and yet they laughed instead of pitying her, and she could not cry; if she had been able to shed tears they would have pitied her she knew, and that horrible laughter would have ceased; but her tears were scorched up with the great heat of the mid-day's sun by the brook.

But why go on! Lucy was in great danger; for many days and nights she was delirious. In her ravings she spoke perhaps of George Berkeley, and of Agnes, and of Edward, but Mrs. Walter was slow of comprehension, for there was no warm affection to quicken her perceptions. If something of the grief which was overwhelming her spirit fell from the burning lips of Lucy, she did but look on it as the common wanderings of delirium, and when she came down from her room she could only say to her husband, in a contented tone—

"Poor thing! she talks all sorts of nonsense— just as I did when I was ill with a fever. But I am not at all alarmed about her; it will soon pass off. I got over my illness very well when I was just about Lucy's age, and I have been quite strong ever since. I am not in the least alarmed about her."

Walter tried to be satisfied, but it was in vain he attempted to read or to attend to parish business, as day after day passed by, and the words " she is much the same," was the answer to his eager inquiry. The doctor had advised perfect quiet, and no one was to enter Lucy's room but those absolutely needed to attend on her; but, at length, Walter could bear it no longer. He stole gently to the door, and stood motionless for minutes together, watching the flushed face and staring eyes of his little suffering sister, then, creeping back to his own study, he locked his door, and the tears stole down his cheeks, and the agonized prayer burst from him—" Save her! oh, my God, save her!"

For awhile Mrs. Walter talked down the doctor; she would not let him tell of danger, and he would not force alarm on those who were unwilling to hear the truth. There was no neglect or injudicious treatment to make it necessary, and there was still some hope of recovery. To do Mrs. Walter justice, she had the merit of being an excellent nurse; no nice sensibility oppressed her; neither hand nor heart trembled, nor did her voice falter with needless anxiety. She was calm, unmoved, matter of fact, and skilful.

The doctor said, "Miss Crofton must be quiet, Miss Crofton must take such and such medicines." Mrs. Walter listened with an unbewildered head, and stuck to the letter of the orders. She was quick, neat, and firm.

But the danger at last became too evident, and too imminent to be longer concealed. Even Mrs. Walter was hushed into fear, and pity, and love. She knew that in all human probability Lucy's life was on its verge. The remembrance of her amiable qualities, her sweet temper under provocation, her cheerfulness, her unobtrusive piety, nay, even her pretty face, her winning ways came to her mind, and with these came also the recollection, on her own side, of unkind words, hard feelings, carelessness about her happiness; and self-reproach swept over that cold, hard heart, and sought out for reprobation every wrong motive, every unworthy action. The new thought arose —was her conduct towards Lucy only what was natural and right? was there any excuse for harshness? was it required?

A chill fell on Mrs. Walter. The thought of questions like these, when there could be no appeal to the world's judgment, made her breathing heavy; tears stood in her eyes, wrung out by the terror and remorse of her heart. It was a great change—would it be lasting? She thought of prayer—she always *said* her prayers night and morning—but now she would pray. She did not kneel, but one fervent prayer for mercy burst from her. Yet she did it in fear; there was not love, there was scarcely faith, she feared too much! but a sort of superstitious comfort crept over her. She walked quietly into Lucy's room again, and dared now to look at the face which had been too terrible to her before. It was very calm, but there were no signs of life.

" Can nothing save her?" thought she, in agony. She went to the room where the doctor was waiting—" Can nothing save her?" she exclaimed, in a voice hoarse with emotion. " Will you try nothing?"

The doctor was touched with distress he so little expected from such a cold, self-possessed person. He entreated her to be calm.

" Indeed there is hope," he said, " but the crisis is not yet arrived. You must rest; I will wait by the bedside, and you, dear madam, must rest yourself;" and Mrs. Walter was left alone, whilst tears came flowing quickly down her cheeks, and she made resolves—alas! that such should be broken!

Walter was now with the doctor in the room of

the patient. Love held the place of remorse in his heart; his pale face showed the mental struggle he was undergoing; his upraised eyes and clasped hands at times told that a strength beyond his own was needed, and was sought in silent prayer.

Yet he, too, had his self-reproaches! Who have not when they think that the time is past in which any omissions in kindness or affection can be repaired? that there are no more days on which that reckoning can be made up? Carelessness, thoughtlessness, undervaluing, hasty words, cold replies—love cannot count the debt which it wishes to have paid, and therefore the sum of omission seems infinite when the book is closed, never more to be opened.

So Walter felt, as he sat watching the face of his little gentle sister. He could think of no neglect on her side. No! the account was all against himself! On her side he remembered only loving words and ways; active charity, warm affection, simple piety. Grief blotted out every fault of hers; there was not one left in his memory to make the thought of losing her more endurable!

CHAPTER XXVIII.

THERE is a sharp ring of the bell in the sitting-room at Woodbine Cottage. Sally came in.

"Eh! Sally, Sally!" said the little lady, holding up a note, "she's worse! Lucy Crofton is worse! Put on your bonnet and shawl and go to the parsonage. See Wilson, if you can, and get the truth. Eh! Sally! Sally! we have known many troubles, but I never thought to have such an one as this to endure! My pretty lamb! She's like a little innocent lamb, Sally! I never loved any one as I have loved her! And I can't get to her! I can't see her! God forgive me for my murmuring! Poor Walter Crofton— poor Walter! And I'm tied hand and foot and can't go to her! Never to see her again! Pretty, loving child! never to see her again!" muttered on the little old lady after Sally left the room, the tears slowly rolling down her cheeks. "And

Walter Crofton—poor Walter! Eh! but his books won't comfort him; and Edward! his broad head never chilled his heart towards that little one! I see his smile now, curling about his lips, as he set a trap for her with his talk, and she would not be trapped, as he knew she would not! but he liked to hear her laugh and scold him in her play as she found him out; and there I sat, like an old ninny, enjoying the fun, as if I was ever likely to enjoy it again; and now there she lies! Ah! who's there? Come in, come in. Ah! if it isn't Barker Preston, sobbing like a child! Why, she's gone! she's gone! I know she is, and he's come to tell me, and to get comfort, poor loving, foolish soul! and how can I give him any! how can I give him any! I who loved her better than any one! Never to see her again! My pretty lamb, my Lucy!"

Whilst Lucy Crofton was lying at the parsonage in danger of life, and those around her were watching anxiously as the hours stole on, giving less and less of hope, in Hulse House there was also a time of trial and of conflict. With equal fallacy to that of the monks of old, Arthur Colville thought that he had entrenched himself around from the intrusion of the world. He had given strict orders to the one trusted confidant, who managed his affairs, and to whom alone the secret of his residence was confided, to destroy at once every letter addressed to him. Hodson had tried to expostulate with his master on a measure which cut off all hope of accidental influence from the remarks and entreaties of friends, or from the chance of his being aroused to fresh sources of interest from the knowledge of events in the world.

But Colville's peremptory tone, as he said— " There must be no communication between me and those I have left. They do not regret me, nor do I regret them," and the harsh, desponding severity of his voice, as he added, " Can I not be freed from importunity unless I lay myself in the grave? There is quiet there!" silenced Hodson.

What if he sought that quiet too soon?

" But what is come over me!" thought Hodson, as this terrible dread glanced through his mind. " How can I fear such sin in my dear master? No, no! it is unjust and wicked even to dream of it for an instant!"

On the evening of the day which we have just described at Hulse Parsonage, Hodson appeared before his master with a letter in his hand. Colville was sitting over a small wood fire, for it was a chilly evening. He glanced angrily at the letter, as he raised his eyes from his book, but before his anger had time to express itself, Hodson explained that the letter was merely a petition from a poor boy, who had so earnestly entreated that the squire should look at it, that Hodson was unwilling to refuse.

"Well," said Colville, his brow clearing, "lay it there; I will look at it presently. You were quite right not to refuse the poor wretch." Hodson laid the letter down; then lingered a little, as if desirous to speak. Colville again looked up.

"Miss Crofton is very ill, sir," Hodson said.

"I know it!" was the cold reply, and after a second's pause, he added, "You told me so before."

Hodson knew that he had named the illness, in the hope of rousing his master to sympathy, but there had been no answer. "And should she die," said Mr. Colville, continuing to speak with as much coldness and severity as ever, "is it such a matter of sorrow that any one should die before they have learnt to regret the day on which they were born?"

"Her brother, sir, is in great affliction."

"Is he selfish, then?" said Mr. Colville: "or does he think that in the future he can shield her from the daily-increasing disappointments and sufferings of existence?" But his tone changed, and he added, with something more of his own natural kindliness, "I am very sorry for Mr. Crofton; he is a good man, and free from all affectation of feeling. His life would be more dreary without his sister's society. Is there any hope of her recovery?" he asked.

Hodson shook his head.

"Indeed it is sad," was Mr. Colville's remark, with far more feeling. There was, perhaps, a reviving recollection of the pleasures of family affection, or of the grief he had himself endured on the loss of his parents, for Arthur Colville's nature had not been hard. It was now embittered, and he affected to despise all the common and natural sources of joy and sorrow. A misdirected and sinful indulgence in his own grief made him careless as to the troubles of others.

When Hodson left him he thought, "Why does any one foolishly expect to be happy? It is a silly struggle! for any reasoning being must be convinced that pain, disappointment, and mortification are the chronic state of every human being. I can pity these poor people, but in doing so, what is it but to murmur against the governing influence which made this suffering a law of being! I am powerless to ward off these miseries! Am I not myself a living witness to their ceaseless thraldom? What if this poor girl recovers! Will she pass her life without adding each day something more to embitter it? Then why should she live? If death does not bring happiness now, why should it do so some years hence?"

And then Colville remembered the letter Hodson had laid beside him. There was a feeling of satisfaction in the idea of his own unselfish benevolence in attending to the requests of the poor, who were to him a privileged race.

"This is a dainty beggar!" he thought, smiling ironically, as he unfolded the dirty outer cover, and came to a neatly folded, well sealed enclosure. He opened it and began to read.

There was complete stillness in the room, except for the ticking of the clock on the mantelpiece. Arthur Colville's hand held the letter—his grasp tightened on it—a mist came over his eyes—paleness over his face. The letter was not a petition from a beggar. It was thus artfully conveyed to ensure its perusal—"I have at last discovered your place of concealment," were the first words, and the handwriting was but too well known to him. In former times it had often brought a thrill of rapture to his heart. But there was a terrible change since those early days of trust and hope! and every relic of the writer had been carefully destroyed. A fierce strife was going on in Arthur Colville's breast as he sat motionless, and pale as death; and then as he started up, a quick flush came to his cheek; the quick flush of anger, and pride, and indignant scorn, spreading up even to his forehead! He paced the room with hasty steps. The letter was clenched in his hand; his angry grasp closed over it; and then, as if not satisfied with this token of contempt and hatred, he tore the paper to pieces; he cast each atom into the fire, and as the flames in turn curled round each word, he watched their demolition with a cruel, scornful pleasure! The first sentence was the only one he had read! Whatever the appeal to his feelings might have been, it was lost! All that it had cost the writer to pen those words was mere wasted pain! The paper on which they had been inscribed was now flickering into a blaze before it crumpled up into a thin, flimsy fragment, which the next draught of air might carry up the chimney. After that evening Hodson observed with pain the increased irritation and depression of his master. There was tenfold bitterness in his tone, and he seemed resolved to bury himself, if possible, more closely than ever.

CHAPTER XXIX.

I MUST again return to the parsonage, where we left the Croftons in great distress and anxiety. For a long time the balance had been wavering between life and death, but at length the scale was turned, and with deep gratitude Walter Crofton heard the words from the lips of the medical man which assured him that the danger was over, and that his sister was restored to him.

It was a fine day in August when Lucy was first carried to the drawing-room. Her sofa was placed near the window, from whence she could see the flowers as they began to glow forth in their gorgeous autumnal colouring. Lucy was pale and delicate; she looked like a slight, fairy being, inspiring a feeling of awe, from her strong contrast to anything of roughness or coarseness. She had never been in the drawing-room since the afternoon in April when she had left it in such gay spirits with Mrs. Berkeley's letter in her hand. Since then how familiar had everything become to her in her room upstairs, where she had first read the letter and known of the sacrifice that was required of her! Even such minute things as the slight variation in the pattern of the paper, the number of scrolls round the frame of a picture, the indistinct letters at the corner of an old print, which she had never observed in health, she knew by heart in her illness.

But these trifles were not the only things that had been learnt by Lucy during her illness, for suffering teaches us much which it is difficult or impossible to learn in health and happiness.

When Lucy first came downstairs after her long illness, her eye rested in turn on each familiar object. She remembered with what a light heart she had run upstairs on that afternoon. She had then known but little of what the sufferings of the mind could be; and yet, much as she had endured, she was able to bless God in her soul for her illness, and for her knowledge of sorrow. Some will say, why is this? Lucy Crofton was an amiable, affectionate girl, with strong religious principle—what did she need more? Ah, how many of us may have felt this of others, or more fatally of ourselves, until affliction has given us a power to understand the deeper things of the spirit! The young man who turned away sorrowful from the call to leave everything and follow Christ, did not know that he needed a higher principle, till the test was applied and he failed. Lucy Crofton little knew how faint was her self-sacrificing love to God, or what it was to feel her own sinfulness—her deep need of the Saviour's atonement, until she was tried through the medium of her earthly affections.

Lucy Crofton had passed through a struggle that had nearly cost her her life, for her love was not lightly given—her feelings were calm, strong, and deep—her love once bestowed, became to her as a sacred, unchanging devotion, to endure through life; and when she was so unexpectedly called upon to relinquish all thoughts of George Berkeley, she did not receive the trial as many girls of her age might have done —with burst of tears and violent agitatation, spending itself in vehement outward distress— but Lucy tried to suppress her emotion, she tried to act deliberately and firmly, on reason and on principle; nor was there any impulse of excitement, or fancied sense of martyrdom, to support her. She saw the full value of what it was she must sacrifice if she agreed to Mrs. Berkeley's request. That "*if*" had often tantalised and bewildered her during the three days which were allowed for deliberation; but at length it was put aside, and she wrote to Mrs. Berkeley agreeing to her request.

Many will doubt whether Lucy's decision was right. We know that it was formed in spite of the earnest pleadings of her own heart, and we can, therefore, admire her heroism of conduct, even if we think her judgment erroneous. To a weaker mind this one act of self-sacrifice would have seemed sufficient, but Lucy felt that she had no right to make the sacrifice at all, without the accompanying resolution that her future life should not be spent in repining, saddening uselessness. There were duties in her home and in her small sphere which must not be neglected; she must be able to share in the joys as well as in the sorrows of others, and, above all, she must strive to gain the spirit of thankfulness and cheerfulness, which was her duty towards God.

She earnestly prayed for help, but sometimes the cry of anguish burst from her lips, and she could scarcely repress the ardent longing that her life might not be prolonged.

There is often a half dreamy state belonging to great bodily weakness, immediately after the cessation of fever, during which there is but little suffering, and as Lucy sank into this state, it seemed to bring repose to her mind, and carried her through the first brunt of her distress. She ceased to think of exertion; she was obliged to rest passively, half sleeping away the hours of the day. But when the powers of thought returned as she grew better, Lucy saw that there had been presumption even in her good resolutions. She saw that a deeper submission was needed, and that she must be content to fail in her attempts to carry out her own high ideas of duty. She must be content to see herself the cause of distress and disappointment to those whom she loved; and still farther, she must learn the lesson that it was not through her own merits, but through her sense of her own weakness and infirmities that she must come to the Saviour and to God through him.

During the first weeks of convalescence, the after-work of illness and sorrow, in the effect on the nerves, is often more difficult to bear than illness itself. There was one trial to Lucy which those alone who have experienced something of it can fully understand, and this was the impossibility of destroying every feeling of hope. She could not persuade herself that, sooner or later, Mrs. Berkeley would not write to release her from her promise, and thus the agitation of suspense, so peculiarly trying to any one whose nerves have been weakened by illness, or by some shock to the feelings, were continued to Lucy day after day. Each afternoon, as the post came in, she grew faint with eagerness to look at the letters, and week after week she turned away with the sickening feeling of disappointment, as the anxiously expected letter never came!

Whilst this languor and depression of spirits lasted, it seemed to Lucy's distorted fancy as if all her usual occupations and objects of interest brought pain with them, and in this state of mind she turned with a strange morbid interest to the thoughts of Hulse House and its melancholy inmate. Walter had confided his fears to her as to Mr. Colville's religious doubts, and these fears had served still more to increase her anxiety about him. There was not excitement enough in the ordinary troubles of life to arouse her feelings. She could sympathise with nothing but deep grief, and the hope of seeing Mr. Colville again, afforded a slight relief to the dreadful monotony of her thoughts, which seemed rubbing and wearing away her heart.

" Ah !" said my sister Jane, "it will be a sad thing if she gets too much interest in Mr. Colville, and I only wish that Mrs. Walter was a more comfortable companion for her. A new, pretty piece of carpet work would have done her good; shading the wools and counting the stitches is very soothing !"

"Perhaps," said Martha, "they had no good shops within reach?" appealing to me, with an apologetic air.

"Probably not," was my answer; "but Barker Preston agreed with Jane that it was a sad thing for Lucy to take too much interest in the recluse, though Lucy little guessed what pain it caused her good-natured friend, nor did she know that he began to look on Mr. Colville as a sort of Bluebeard in disguise."

My sister Martha slightly started.

"Were all the rooms at Hulse House constantly unlocked and dusted by the housemaids?" she asked, anxiously.

I shook my head.

" I really could not say that they were." Martha and Jane looked at one another, but

Martha turned the subject as too painful to be dwelt upon, and asked me what Barker Preston felt during Lucy's illness and danger.

"It is not easy to describe his distress," I said.

His only consolation had been in hovering about the parsonage on the chance of seeing Walter Crofton or his wife, or of catching the doctor, or gleaning a ray of hope from the faces of the servants or villagers; but, above all, in going to talk with Miss Walcott, over and over again, of Lucy's perfections.

When he was at last allowed to see Lucy, he crept into the drawing-room on tiptoes, on purpose to make as little noise as his creaking boots would allow; but the cheerful face which he proposed to wear for the sake of "brisking her up," as he called it, was a complete failure, for as he first caught sight of her pale face and large, melancholy eyes, he was entirely overcome! His countenance fell—the words of welcome died on his lips—all he could do was to take Lucy's little wasted hand in both of his and say not a word!

As Lucy grew stronger he recovered his powers of whistling and eating his dinner, until her eager excited attention at the accidental mention of Mr.

Colville's name caused a fresh anxiety. His appetite again failed him, his whistling ceased, whilst his perplexity how to save her from the fascinations of the recluse became greater than ever.

Meantime we have seen that Mr. Colville's despondency had been deepening, and as he came forward to meet Walter Crofton on their first interview in the library at Hulse House after Lucy's illness, his figure was bent, as if from age; his eyes looked sunken and hollow, and his brown waving hair was slightly sprinkled with gray.

CHAPTER XXX.

There had been much gloom over the parsonage, and now there was a shadow even over Woodbine Cottage.

"I do not like to vex you, ma'am," were the words of Miss Walcott's maid one day to her little mistress; "but, as you say, ma'am, truth is always better than falsehood, I will tell you the real truth. Mrs. Wilson says to me, when I went last to the parsonage, 'Sally,' says she, 'Miss Lucy does not get on a bit, and what's more, it's my opinion she never will."

Miss Walcott looked up, and hemmed and fidgetted. "What does the doctor say, Sally?"

"Says he hopes she will be better. I hate *hopes*, ma'am! They always mean something dreadful when a doctor speaks of them."

Miss Walcott might have given a little short laugh, had she been happy enough for it.

"Well, well! Sally! people are mistaken sometimes! Let us say no more about it! Vexed! Yes, to be sure I am vexed, but stick to the truth, Sally, for all that!"

Miss Walcott could not recover her good-humour, and she was not at all better when the door bell rang about an hour or two afterwards.

"What is that noise?" she said, sharply. "Whistling! I hate whistling!" Barker Preston," she said, before he was half in the room, "what do you come whistling up my stairs for? Don't you know I hate that silly noise men contrive to screw out of their mouths, just to prove they are inferior to women? And there you are, coming in with your dirty shoes, making a mess in my room, and whistling as if there was nobody ill in the world!"

"Hang the shoes and the whistling!" exclaimed Barker Preston, "I forgot all about them, for I have such capital news from the parsonage! I have been sitting with her, Miss Walcott, and she has been laughing! And I met the doctor, and he said, 'Mr. Preston, Miss Crofton is getting on rarely now! We shall see her out of doors very soon.'"

"Now God be praised!" said the little lady, her eyes brightening. "Whistle away, Barker

Preston! Go through the whole opera of Don Giovanni, if you like! Whistle away as much as you please, and wipe your shoes on my carpet every day of the year, if you like! Here, Sally had been telling me a cock-and-a-bull story of what Wilson said, and what she said to her, till I was as cross and as sore as if I had been beaten! Whistle away, Barker Preston, but tell me first all she said and looked."

Barker Preston said, " Ay! I knew you would be pleased, and I will tell you all about it. After I had been there a little time, she said (Miss Crofton I mean), Mr. Preston (she calls me Mr. Preston, you know), Mr. Preston, give my love to Miss Walcott, and tell her I hope to come and see her very soon; and then she smiled, and I said something, and then she laughed—a real, downright laugh!"

Miss Walcott blew her nose violently and muttered something about "an old fool," and cleared her throat, and then said " I am very glad to hear this! That child, Lucy Crofton at the parsonage, is a particular favourite of mine, Barker Preston. She is a good girl. I never saw a wrong twist in her in my life. If you put a straight line before her, she would not shut one eye and then say it was crooked, but she would look steadily at it with both eyes open, and she would see exactly whether it was straight, or whether it curved ever so little, but she would not bother you by telling about the curve if there was no need for it."

"That's just it!" said Barker Preston, with enthusiasm. "If it was an ugly day of bad sport, and everybody out of humour, she would not go and poke it at you, when you were in for it, that you would not find all day, and yet she would see it sharper than any one!"

"And so she smiled, did she?" said Miss Walcott, after a short pause of consideration.

"Smiled! bless you! she laughed!" said Barker Preston.

"Some people are very pretty, Miss Walcott," he said, after a pause.

"I should think there was something newer to find out than that!" said Miss Walcott, with her short, chuckling laugh.

"I am very glad," said my sister Jane, "that she is getting better, and I hope Mrs. Walter will send her out in the carriage on the first fine day."

"A visit to Miss Walcott," said my sister Martha, "is what I should strongly recommend."

"And," said I, "that is exactly what she is thinking about at this moment. She is actually in the carriage, on her way to Woodbine Cottage, and little Miss Walcott is becoming quite restless and nervous with the expectation of seeing her."

"Now, Sally," she said to her maid, "don't start and cry out, 'Eh! dear! Miss Crofton, how ill you look!' but receive her as if she had been sitting here as usual every week in the last three months! People are weak and nervous after a bad illness, and if they are flurried by silly remarks they can't get over it. There she is, Sally! there she is!" she exclaimed, in a quick tone. "I see the carriage just by the elm tree. Remember, Sally! don't say so much as 'I hope you are better, Miss Crofton,' for if you do, I'll send you off at a month's notice, without your Christmas gown and cap! Come in, Lucy, my dear; I was just expecting you, and there is the sofa ready for you. I wanted some one to talk to. I hate being silent, my tongue gets so stiff! I can chatter on to exercise it while you rest. I have had no one but Sally to speak to all the morning."

"How pleasant this is," said Lucy, as she lay quietly on the sofa, looking at her dear little Miss

Walcott. The white cap looked cleaner, and droller, and more enlivening than ever.

"Yes, child!" said Miss Walcott, twitching away at her netting. "Yes, child! it is a comfortable thing to have you here. I like talking to you, for I know you pick up my meaning clean and tidy, and I can say just what I please, without stopping to think whether you will wonder or blunder about it." And so the little lady chattered on till she saw that Lucy had recovered from her first nervousness, and then she asked a few questions and led her to talk, and Lucy went home at the end of two hours with more cheerfulness and composure than she had felt since her illness.

CHAPTER XXXI.

But to Mrs. Walter Crofton, what was the sunshine of a cottage compared to the grand obscurity of a great house? She hurried into the drawing-room at the Parsonage, one day, not long after Lucy's first visit to Woodbine Cottage, with a joyful exclamation.

"Mr. Colville is coming, Lucy! I saw him riding up to the gate. I hope you will not mind being left alone, for I have so much to do in the village that I must run away at once! If you are tired, you can ring for Wilson to help you to your room."

Mr. Colville had not seen Lucy since her illness—he was not an observant person, for he was habitually self-engrossed—but something in her look arrested his attention. Sorrow and agitation may seem to pass and to be forgotten, but they leave an ineffaceable stamp, on the expression as well as on the heart and character. It was not only that Lucy was pale and delicate in appearance from the effects of illness, but there rested on her countenance that shadow—soft, and even grand as it may be—which is first spread over it by the knowledge of sorrow, and the work of endurance going on in the soul.

Mr. Colville almost started as he saw her, and perhaps there was, to such a mind as his, a kind of satisfaction in the conviction that she had been unhappy. He saw in her, for the first time, a person who would be able to understand him. It was evident that, as in his own case, some sorrow had fallen on her, early in life, before the feelings had undergone the deadening process of time.

After a little conversation, he took up a volume of Coleridge's Poems which lay on the table, and he asked Lucy, with an air of some inquisitiveness, whether she had read them.

"Not lately," was her answer.

"You were perhaps afraid of them?" he said. "When we are happy, and can shake off the vague images of distress which he delights to create, it is very well to indulge in these fanciful horrors, but it is not so safe or pleasant when the mind has too much of its own gloom."

Lucy looked up with a surprised, inquiring look. She had not told Mr. Colville she had been unhappy. How had he guessed it? She was anxious he should go on.

"The chimera of hopefulness should be detained as long as possible," he added. "There is a further stage of suffering, where hope takes to itself wings, and refuses to remain."

"But why should we have to reach that stage at all?" said Lucy, eagerly.

"Why?" exclaimed Mr. Colville. "Do you then really suppose that after the first effervescence of youthful spirits has ceased, there are any who, if they confessed the truth, are not bowed down with the cares and disappointment of every day and every hour of their existence?"

"Nay, but," said Lucy, "I have seen many who have even had great afflictions, and who have passed through them, and have lived in cheerfulness and happiness to old age!"

"Is it really so?" said Mr. Colville, ironically; "or rather is it a finer species of deception? If those of whom you speak are mere placid specimens—the mental zoophytes, as it were, of humanity—it is absurd to treat of them. I am not thinking of the mere *animal* man! I speak of those who have genius and intellect—ardent affection, sensitive natures!—those with whom the clay is over-balanced and annihilated by the spirit, not the spirit outweighed and smothered by the clay! A more common case!" was added, with his frequent, querulous, half-sneering tone. "But look to a mind," he continued, for whom Coleridge would write, and by whom he would hope to be understood, and then tell me whether the depths of which I am speaking will not most sadly and surely arrive for him!"

"You would take away all comfort," said Lucy, and her hands fell listlessly at her side, and the tears were in her eyes; for as her own mind was still in an unhealthy state, she felt overwhelmed by the influence of his despondency, even though she wished him to go on speaking. He was turning over the leaves of the volume of Coleridge.

"Do you know this passage?" he said, and then, in a voice of great sweetness, he read these lines—

"'Like one that on a lonesome road
  Doth walk in pain and dread,
And having once turned round walks on
  And turns no more his head,
Because he knows a frightful fiend
  Doth close behind him tread.'

This is but an image of the mind's pain and

dread; and who can dare to speak of comfort when the wickedness or the misery of almost every human being around us are the frightful fiends constantly possessing and invading the mind!" Mr. Colville's manner had lost its taunting tone, and had become more earnest, and turning suddenly to Lucy, and looking at her as he had never done before, he said, almost with emotion, "Is this language strange to you, Miss Crofton, or do I guess rightly? Since we last met, it is easy to perceive that we have more in common. Why I speak of it I scarcely know; but you will believe that it is not from mere vulgar curiosity or inquisitiveness into the cause of your grief!" and he paused, as if it were for her answer.

There is certainly something in our nature which seems to constitute sorrow as the strongest bond of sympathy between human beings. Lucy would never have dreamt of making a confidant of Mr. Colville if she had been happy, but now she scarcely felt any hesitation in answering to his appeal; her face was paler for a minute, and then a flush passed over it, as she said, "No one knows or guesses it; but you are right!"

"Brother!" said my sister Martha, sternly,

"brother! no woman ought to love an unbeliever."

"Only pity him?" said Jane, gently and inquiringly, looking rather timidly, first at Martha and then at me.

"Only pity him," I said, for I did not wish just then to enter into a discussion on the distinction between love and Christian charity.

"Very well," said Martha, in a satisfied tone, "she must only pity him:" upon which, as I saw that my horse was waiting for me, I wished my sisters good-bye and set off on my solitary ride; and then I remembered that I had given the reader but a very vague idea of the reasons for Mrs. Berkeley's letter to Lucy Crofton, and as I have no object in concealing them I will go back a little to relate something of her wishes and plans for her son George, which his attachment to Lucy Crofton had seemed doomed to thwart.

Near the country home of the Berkeleys, which was a fine old stately place, with all the proper appurtenances of avenues, deer park, and large manorial hall, there was an old baronial hall, equally gifted with avenues and deer park, and here lived two excellent people, Lord and Lady Raymond. Their only son had died in childhood, and there were only two daughters left to inherit all the stately possessions of the house of Raymond.

With true womanly ingenuity, Mrs. Berkeley formed a plan that her second son George should marry the Raymonds' second daughter, Margaret. We know Mrs. Berkeley's character. What Lady Raymond thought of, in her gentleness, as a very nice scheme, provided " *dear George* " took a fancy to " *dearest Margaret,*" Mrs. Berkeley settled with all the determination of pride.

Mrs. Berkeley had been left a widow very early in life. Her husband had given a proof of the boundless respect and admiration he had felt for her by leaving his younger son dependent on her during her lifetime. If he married without her consent she could withhold from him the addition to his fortune which would alone enable him to maintain a wife.

Mrs. Berkeley felt that she had a perfect right to dispose of her children's lives and loves as she thought best for them. She had remarkably strong prejudices respecting aristocratic birth, and I can well imagine with what a clash her mind was stunned, when, instead of the high-born Margaret, the daughter of her hopes, for whom she had in secret destined her son George, he proposed to her the sister of a poor country clergyman, a person, too, whose family she believed had been in trade! In her eyes there was a broad distinctive line between the little set in London, amongst whom she lived and to which she belonged, and all the outer world; and this, blended with her exclusive feelings as to high birth, formed, in her mind, an impassable barrier between the one and the other. The evils of the Crofton connection had been exaggerated. She was told that trade had soiled the fingers of Lucy's father, instead of that very mild infusion of its pollutions, in the person of Lucy's grandmother, which was really the case. Could George, her own aristocratic son, ever be happy with a wife whose very smiles might have a gleam of the counter in them? Would there not be constant pain to his refined mind when he saw in the family quarterings the cottony shade smothering the shields of knights and squires of old, who had nobly worked at nothing! How could he walk in his father's halls without a blush on his check! Mrs. Berkeley could not reason against such objections! Her own cheek glowed with proud indignation and mortification, and she felt but little consideration due to the upstart aspirations of one of the *canaille,* such as Lucy Crofton.

But Mrs. Berkeley had only earned her son's consent to a year's silence on the condition that she would at once sanction their marriage and contribute the necessary addition to his income, if he still desired to marry Lucy on his return, and he was then free to declare his feelings to her at once. That this contingency might never arrive, she wrote her letter to Lucy Crofton, and as she did so, she believed that the time would come when her son would thank her for having saved him from such a *mesalliance.* But there was another objection, which at present must appear to her son more reasonable, and which, in fact, there was no reasoning against! As his own fortune was far too small to enable him to marry, he must be aware that at this moment of pecuniary difficulty she could not deprive herself of the means to enable him to marry against her wishes! A year's delay had been gained, and Lucy's consent to her request made it probable that this year might be lengthened into the "for ever," to which Lucy's heart had at last acquiesced.

Whether Mrs. Berkeley would have written her letter to Lucy, proud and unreasonable as she was, but for the strong pressure of a nervous illness we cannot pretend to say! It was so entirely unwarrantable that we cannot believe she would have made such an extraordinary demand under other circumstances; but, like other fancies imbibed during mental excitement or delirium, it stamped itself on the mind with unusual force, and she did not retract when she partially recovered her health, because she never learnt to view it but through the false medium under which the idea had been originated. Her saner and better judgment was therefore unable to act upon it.

When the year of George Berkeley's absence was past, Lucy heard of his return to England, but this was all. His mother's sentence then had gone forth, and he had obeyed. Was it weakness or indifference? It mattered not, she was left to her fate! The only intelligence she received was an accidental careless one in a letter from Agnes Spencer. After naming the Digbys, she said, "Digby Manor reminds me that your former admirer, George Berkeley, is at home again. There has been much trouble in the family. His brother Frederic got involved in some of those horrid speculations about which we are all running mad, and poor Mrs. Berkeley has had a dreadful nervous illness."

"Your former admirer!" These words looked strange to one whose love for him had caused her such deep unhappiness! Agnes was ignorant of the truth, and Lucy knew that she was, but she could not shake off the influence of this careless sentence. It conveyed to her a lonely sense that all the interest George Berkeley had ever felt for her was in the past, and that even then it had been just that sort of passing admiration which was a fitting subject for good-humoured raillery and nothing more.

CHAPTER XXXII.

In the present day it is the fashion to make such a minute analysis of our feelings, that there is perhaps a danger of having no feelings left! As I am an old-fashioned person, I shall say no more of Lucy Crofton's feelings, but leave them in that quiet, sanctified retirement, which she would have expected and desired for them; as her health became stronger, she gave the best proof that sorrow had improved instead of embittering her nature, by her kind and unselfish cheerfulness, and her increased solicitude for the comfort and happiness of all around her; and when, with painful rapidity, after George Berkeley's return to England, a rumour reached her that he was engaged to marry Miss Margaret Raymond, I am not going to relate how she received this report. All I know is, that Barker Preston became suddenly very anxious and unhappy about her, and assured Miss Walcott that people sometimes went into rapid declines, and that it was usually the best people who did so.

They were not perhaps exactly these thoughts, but something more general of the distresses and uncertainties of life, which occupied Lucy one morning after this rumour had performed its work of annoyance.

Mrs. Walter had gone out for a day's shopping to the neighbouring town; and Lucy was sitting alone, looking vacantly and cheerlessly on the flower garden, which used to be her delight, when she was startled by the servant's opening the door, and without a moment in which to collect her thoughts, George Berkeley was before her. She could have screamed with agitation and surprise, but she controlled herself.

George Berkeley came up to her. An exclamation of distress burst from him, as he saw the change which illness and sorrow had effected.

"You have been ill, Miss Crofton!" he said. "You have been ill, and I knew nothing of it! Why did I not hear of this?"

"Yes! I have been ill," Lucy said, in a faint voice. She could not utter a word more—she dared not look up.

"You have been ill, and I knew nothing of it!" George Berkeley exclaimed again, with unmistakeable tenderness in his tone and look, but with increasing agitation; he said something about having been kept away—about "a cruel separation"—but it was all confusion to Lucy, and to him it seemed little less so.

At length he got up; he went to the window; then returned to the seat by Lucy, and said, "It is useless trying to conceal what I feel. At the risk of startling you by my abruptness, I must speak." And then in plain, earnest, manly language, George Berkeley poured forth to Lucy the expression of his love. He told her of his past difficulties; he told her that since his return from abroad he had been kept watching by the sick bed of his mother; that the moment he could safely leave her he came—not waiting for a fresh permission from her, as he dared not agitate her by speaking on a subject of so much interest,—but he came at once to Lucy to know his fate, to ask if she could love him—to ask if she would consent to be his wife. He appealed to her for an answer—her hand was clasped in his.

And Lucy, poor Lucy! what was she to say? Her great and unchanging affection for George Berkeley was vehement at her heart; but the recollection of Mrs. Berkeley's letter, and her own fatal promise, rested there also, like a dead weight. George Berkeley brought her no release! all that he said made this certain! Her agitation and distress were too great for control. She scarcely knew what were the words she uttered, or what she ought to have uttered. She only felt that her lover was before her, her hand clasped in his, and that she loved him more than ever; and as he repeated his eager, passionate appeal to her, asking her whether she could love him, she exclaimed,

"Oh! why will you ask me? It is too late!— too late! Nay," she added, as her face crimsoned over with a bright blush, "not too late to say that I love you, for why should I conceal it? It may be a comfort to you in our separation, to know that I love you. But it is too late, too late!" she repeated, half wildly.

"Why do you say this?" said George Berkeley, passionately kissing the hand still clasped in his. "You have owned that you love me! Do we not love one another?—do you doubt my love?"

"Oh! no, no!" exclaimed Lucy. "But it is too late—I have promised!"

George Berkeley started and drew back.

"Yes," said Lucy, "I have promised! I told you it was too late."

"Promised!—promised!" said George Berkeley, recoiling. "But you love me?" he added, and his voice was almost stern.

"Oh! do not ask me that again!" said Lucy, the blood rushing to her face, and then leaving her pale as death. "I was weak and wicked to say it! I can tell you nothing! Only leave me! you must leave me! I have been very weak—but I have been ill! I was almost gone! Oh, if I had died then, what sorrow would have been spared me! But this is wicked! very wicked! I hardly know what I am saying!" Lucy made a violent effort to speak more calmly. "You must leave me, Mr. Berkeley," she said, "for I can tell you nothing. I would ask you to love me still, but that it would be wrong, for we must not meet again."

"Not meet again!" exclaimed George Berkeley. "Good God! What is it? What can you mean?"

"Oh! do not ask me," said Lucy," with increasing agitation. "Pray do not ask me! Only leave me at once, and do not reproach me. I have suffered so much, and now......" Lucy's voice ceased. She had fainted.

George Berkeley rang for help. The maid

was sent for. Lucy was carried upstairs. George Berkeley waited below in a state of anguish hardly to be described. Was Lucy false? Was she engaged to another? Barker Preston had sometimes spoken to him mysteriously about Mr. Colville, the recluse, but he had only laughed at the idea; for the last days spent at Fernmere with Lucy had removed almost every doubt as to his love being returned. But now Barker Preston's hints recurred to him. Could it be true? Could he have misinterpreted her looks and words? or could her sister-in-law have involved her in an engagement contrary to her own wishes? But then what did her avowal of love mean? Was it possible that Lucy Crofton, who was so modest, and gentle, and pure in thought, should avow her love for him, if she were engaged to another? The maid returned.

"How is Miss Crofton?" was his eager question.

"She is better, sir. She desired me to give you this note, and to tell you she was better."

The maid left the room. George Berkeley tore open the note. There were only these few words—

"I entreat of you, if you have ever loved me,

not to remain here. I cannot explain. You must not ask it, but leave me at once, and may God's blessing be with you now and for ever!"

"LUCY CROFTON."

George Berkeley left the house. He saw that there was nothing to be done but to submit. For Lucy's sake he must obey her earnest request, but afterwards this mystery must be solved! He returned to watch again the alternations of his mother's health. Her nervous excitement had scarcely abated, and it was impossible to tell her what had passed between Lucy and himself. And indeed it seemed useless to do so. He little knew why Lucy had rejected him, and it seemed cruel to run the risk of agitating his mother unless for some obvious reason. But to submit passively, and ignorantly to renounce the love which had been so precious to him, the reader will easily believe was the farthest possible thing from his intentions, and Mrs. Berkeley little guessed what was going on in her son's mind as she comfortably reposed in the belief that he had conquered his attachment, because he never spoke to her about it! As she was not anxious to pique him into a revival of his affection, the subject was never named between them.

CHAPTER XXXIII.

This great trial in Lucy's life was over! Whether she had been right or wrong in making the promise to Mrs. Berkeley, she had been firm in keeping it.

I will not string together a set of words about broken hearts and blighted affections. It is easy to imagine Lucy Crofton's distress when George Berkeley was once more before her, and he poured forth the story of his love, and of the hopes on which he had been building so fondly during their long separation, and she could say nothing to him! she could only entreat him to leave her—without a word of explanation. She let him go away supposing her capricious, perhaps disgusted at her strange conduct, and deeply wounded by her cruel rejection.

The tone of his voice, the look of pain on his face as she begged him to leave her, were often terribly present with Lucy as every particular of the short, agitating interview was constantly being re-enacted in her mind.

But I will dwell no longer on the past. One era of Lucy's life was over, and we may now think of her as setting out again on her journey through life, feeling as if the rest of the way must be only a grave, sad struggle with the difficulties and duties on her road, and intermixed with very little pleasure or amusement; although she owned it might be with much sober happiness and peace. But, in spite of strong religious trust and joy, life, in itself, was a new and a wearisome thing to her; and yet to the common observer it seemed to pass on just as before at Hulse Parsonage. Poor Miss Crofton had had a dangerous illness, and she looked very delicate; but then she was young, she had nothing to trouble her, and no doubt she would soon get back her pretty colour, and regain her strength.

Happily for Lucy, the medical man saw deeper into the matter than her relations and neighbours did. He saw she would sink away but for some change, and he peremptorily ordered her to the sea-side. Lucy went; thorough change of scene was of use; and when she returned home she was really better in health and in nerves.

It would have been more agreeable to Lucy's feelings never to have gone into society again; she was not in the habit of analysing every motive with microscopic exactness, but she was under the habitual guidance of broad unwavering principles of right and wrong, and she could find no plea for refusing all sympathy or communion with her richer neighbours, any more than with her poorer ones. So she conquered her indolence and her repugnance to society, and when she was required to go out again with her brother and Mrs. Walter, she neither dissolved into floods of tears, nor drew down her face into sanctimonious disapproval; but she put on her nicest dress, and tried to enter cheerfully into the interests and pleasures of others.

"Tears are very damaging to handsome silks and velvets!" said my sister Martha. "It was very right of Lucy to restrain them."

"Very right, for many reasons," I said: "silks and velvets inclusive, if you please."

The greatest trial in the line of social duties, was the first visit to Digby Manor.

The day was now come, for Walter and his wife and Lucy were driving along the road that led to the Digbys, and Agnes Spencer was to be there. Lucy wondered how she should bear it if Agnes should fix her piercing eyes upon her and jest about old times, and speak of "her former admirer."

But just then the old gray chimneys of Hulse House appeared in sight, as they drove along the road, and Lucy's mind was diverted from her own troubles to those of the unhappy recluse. His religious doubts, in contrast with her own settled trust and faith, seemed more fearful and terrible each time she thought of it; but then the hope came over her that Mr. Colville's conversations with Walter must at length have some effect, and that even his acquaintance with her brother, and his knowledge of Walter's unselfish character, and active, consistent piety could not fail in time to have a useful influence.

The dark side of the view had vanished; and as Lucy again looked at the gray chimneys and the high boundary wall, she smiled. Mrs. Walter observed it.

" Ah !" she thought, " Hulse House is the best cure ! I see that ! much better than fidgetting off to the sea-side !" And then Mrs. Walter's ideas took a new direction, and she wondered aloud, with some little peevishness, whether " *that Mr.*

Berkeley" would be at Digby Manor. " He called and ran away in such an abrupt way the day you fainted, you know, Lucy. I am sure he must have tired you. He talks a great deal at times."

These words sounded strange to Lucy; but she tried to harden herself to the accidental mention of George Berkeley's name. It was a name remembered daily in her prayers; while to her sister-in-law he was only "that Mr. Berkeley!"

At length they were at Digby Manor. Agnes Spencer came eagerly forward to meet them. But she was so much affected by the change which illness and sorrow had made on the happy little Lucy Crofton she had last seen, that tears rushed into her eyes.

"Dear Lucy!" were all the words that she could utter for an instant; as she put her arms fondly round her, and kissed her affectionately.

"My dear Miss Crofton," said Mrs. Digby, "do tell me all about your illness! I hope you got our inquiries? We sent constantly."

Lucy thanked Mrs. Digby, and Mrs. Walter assured her the kind messages had been duly delivered. Agnes saw Lucy's varying colour, and she released her from Mrs. Digby and Mrs. Walter.

" There is a large party here," she said, " and

as we must make ourselves smart for the evening, let us come upstairs at once. Mrs. Digby, can you tell me which is Lucy's room?"

"Oh!" said Mrs. Digby, "Miss Crofton always has 'the Rose Chintz!' It is called by her name; our Rosebud, you know," she added, affectionately.

"Some of our party are not strangers to you," she said, turning expressly to Lucy. "Mr. Fitzgerald and Lord Englefield are old acquaintances, I know."

"Oh! Lord Englefield," said Mrs. Walter, who immediately heard the name, "he is a very agreeable person. You know, Lucy, we met him here two or three years ago."

Mrs. Digby glanced at Lucy. She expected to see an animated look of pleasure, for Lord Englefield's admiration had been very evident; but the only change in Lucy's face was a passing contraction of the brow, as a sudden pang of recollection shot through her.

Having thought so long of Lucy Crofton, under the solemn tutelage of illness and of grief, I can scarcely fancy her again in the clatter of the surface-life of society: with all its seeming heartlessness, society forms a useful element in our training; if it calms down enthusiasm, it also dispels unprofitable sentiment; with its sharp touches of actual annoyance, it rudely awakens us from morbid gloom, much as if a muddy cart suddenly came in contact with a despairing youth who was preparing to drown his sorrows in a watery grave. He would probably jump away from the cart as briskly as if he had not been utterly reckless of every personal consideration an instant before!

To compare small things with great, the cart was something like the assemblage of unromantic guests at Digby Manor, with whom Lucy Crofton was brought in contact. Amongst them was that crafty statesman—the Earl of Longville, with a shrewd head and a cool heart—and his daughters, the Ladies Frances and Emily Longville, with soft tender hearts and unreasoning heads; Mr. Fairfax—a very clever, but rather cynical elderly man; Lord George Bolton—a merry youth, who took life with good-humoured alacrity; Mr., Mrs., and Miss Howard, and Mr. Henry Dalton, whose bride elect was the amiable, pretty Miss Howard. The Ladies Longville expressed themselves enchanted to see "dear Miss Spencer;" but they privately wondered what "papa would think if they behaved as independently and talked as much as she did." They spoke of her friend, Miss Crofton, as "a darling little thing," with her pretty *naïve* simplicity! about which everyone raved. They privately expressed their doubts whether she really was *so very* simple. Perhaps she knew, as well as others, that Lord Englefield was the best *parti* in London. Still she was quite a little angel!

On coming to Digby Manor that afternoon, Lord Englefield felt a good deal of excitement on hearing that Lucy Crofton was one of the expected guests. Mrs. Digby told him that Lucy had had a dangerous illness. He was sufficiently mortified with the repulse he had met with from her when they last met, to make him hope that her attractions had lessened; and as she came into the room before dinner-time, he looked at her critically, to try and discover a fault. But, alas! he could only confess that there was an increased charm in the soft dreamy paleness of her countenance. He sauntered towards her as dinner was announced: her coldness must be forgiven; and he was going to make the grand mistake of offering his arm to take her in to dinner, when his wiser judgment showed him that a little seeming neglect was the better plan, so he did not avoid Lady Frances Longville, who sat anxiously, *perfectly indifferent,* waiting for him. He talked hunting-talk across her, most of the dinner-time, to Mr. Henry Dalton; but Lady Frances assured Mrs. Digby, nevertheless, that Lord Englefield had been "so agreeable."

"You think Lord Englefield so agreeable, Lady Frances?" exclaimed Miss Spencer, who unluckily for her had overheard the remark.

"Oh! Miss Spencer," said Lady Frances, "you are so fastidious; you think no one agreeable. Now I do think poor Lord Englefield......"

"Rich Lord Englefield! you mean," interrupted Agnes; "and, after all, I do love rich people myself! There is a sort of good-humoured complacency about them; they bear the privations of life so well for others! They recommend to their poor friends some indispensable luxury, with so much kindness! They are sure a drive in a carriage and four, on a fine day, would exactly suit some poor woman who has been longing all her life for the one-horse *chay* she can't afford to have; and they beg a young lady, who comes out in her best muslin gown, made by mamma's maid at home, to employ Madame A——, as much less expensive than Madame B——; and they are *so* good-natured about it!"

"Oh! that is exactly true," said Lady Frances Longville. "I remember Lady Brighton telling me, at my first ball, that I must get my dresses from Madame D——; and papa quite raved at the idea of our employing such an expensive milliner."

"Ah!" said Agnes, with a curl on her lip, as she sat down by Lucy, while Lady Frances turned to Mrs. Digby, for a little refreshing talk about ball-dresses.

"Who is that lovely little creature?" said Lord George Bolton, on coming in to the drawing-room after dinner, to Lady Emily Longville, as he looked at Lucy.

"Oh! Lord George, pray don't talk so loud. She will certainly hear you, poor little thing."

"Ah! ah! ah!" laughed Lord George, who was always amused at everything. "And what if she did, Lady Emily? Does not every one like to be called a lovely creature!"

Lord George was soon introduced to Lucy, and insisted on teaching her a new game at cards; and his assurance that there was no gambling in it, of course, warranted another laugh.

We, many of us, know what it is to return to society after a long interval of illness or affliction. We are at first half bewildered by the ceaseless noise of voices and the apparent gaiety of every one around us. We can scarcely believe that any one but ourselves has ever had a sorrow, or could ever have known what illness or affliction meant, and that we shall ever again become as gay and careless as this talkative assemblage, seems impossible!

This was Lucy's feeling that evening, and she would have been surprised had she heard Lord George Bolton's exclamation to Mrs. Digby, as he followed her into the next room, towards the close of it.

"Oh, Mrs. Digby! you have the pleasantest parties I ever knew. As to Miss Crofton, she is quite a gem. Englefield, what do you think I call Miss Crofton? Ha! ha! ha!"

"Lord George!" said Lady Frances Longville, who just then glided near them, "what can you be laughing at?"

"Oh, a hundred things!" said Lord George. "I hardly know what at this moment."

"Nay," said Lord Englefield, rather stiffly; "Miss Crofton was your last subject."

When I reached this point in my story, I found my sister Martha beginning to doubt the merits of constancy. Lord Englefield was evidently an agreeable and amiable young man. Lucy Crofton ought not to throw away her chance of extensive usefulness, as a rich man's wife, because of an attachment, which by this time had better be buried in oblivion.

During the next few days, I said, Lord Englefield's admiration for Lucy increased as much as her best friends could desire.

Lord Englefield had began on the neglectful plan; but if Lucy did not tire of it, he certainly did before the next day was over, although his recollection of Lucy's former repulse made him guarded in his attentions, and he tried to merge the lover for the present in the agreeable companion. Lord Englefield had many good qualities, and a very winning refinement and charm of manner; he succeeded so well in his attempts to please Lucy, that Lady Emily Longville sometimes begged Lord George Bolton to look how prettily Miss Crofton was smiling at him! which generally caused a hearty laugh from Lord George, and a speedy attempt to gain some of Lucy's smiles for himself.

There is no occasion to discuss the occupations and the conversations of the large party at Digby Manor. There was much clever conversation going on between Agnes Spencer, Walter Crofton, Mr. Fairfax, and Mr. Fitzgerald; with interludes of more ponderous *persiflage* from others; and some dry discussions between Lord Longville and Mr. Digby. Meantime Mr. Henry Dalton could sit peacefully by his pretty little bride elect, and whisper to her of their happy prospects.

Lucy happened to look at them, and sigh with a momentary feeling of envy. Lord Englefield, who was constantly watching her, unluckily observed it.

"Have you ever thought of envying those two happy people?" he said, in a low voice, slightly glancing at the lovers.

Lucy could not honestly say "No." "I suppose that every one likes to see happiness," was her guarded reply.

"Then," said Lord Englefield, with a look of meaning, "you acknowledge that it is happiness to be so situated?"

"It is but fair to suppose people happy who tell you they are so!" said Lucy, with as much carelessness as she could assume.

"There must be great degrees of happiness," said Lord Englefield, still persevering on that subject, and with so much meaning in his look and manner, that Lucy became determined to stop him at the risk of apparent rudeness, so she got up and said, with a smile,

"That little knot of talkers certainly seem very

happy; I must go and listen to what they are saying."

Lord Englefield bit his lip. Was it a *ruse?* or was it real unwillingness to receive his addresses? His admiration had ripened into a good healthy, hearty love, strong enough to bear down every selfish whisper as to loss of liberty, and he had settled some hours before that a marriage with Lùcy would be the perfection of happiness; her consent alone was wanting!

The chance of being refused was not one of the doubts Lord Englefield had been apt to entertain, but Lucy was teaching him to be diffident; and he felt a strong suspicion that she would reject him. He feared that there was another attachment. How must he find out? Miss Spencer was the most likely person to help him, and he tried to sound her on the subject. Agnes was animated by a wicked little spirit of mischief as she discovered his object. Courted and flattered as he was by the world, she thought a rebuff would be rather salutary; so she lulled him into security by receiving his cautious leading questions very carelessly, and then, having made him secure, she let him run along the line.

" Miss Crofton, I suppose, is engaged? Is not

she?" he said, as if it were a matter of complete indifference to himself.

"I don't think so," said Agnes.

"Really!" was the animated reply. "But she has many admirers?"

"Oh! yes," said Agnes.

"Yes?" repeated Lord Englefield, less gaily. "And who, then, is the favoured one who is likely to ease Mrs. Crofton of her *chaperonage?*"

"It is easy to guess at some of her admirers," said Agnes, her eyes twinkling under the dear delight of teasing, "but it is not right to talk about them. However, perhaps, you have heard of some new one?"

"*Some* of her admirers!" thought Lord Englefield, with a much saddened feeling. "Oh!" he said, in a tone of pique, "I have no doubt that there are a whole host of first, second, and third cousins dying for love of her, but the only one I have heard of as likely to be successful is a neighbour, Mrs. Crofton spoke of. These things always interest one, you know, Miss Spencer!"

"Oh! yes," said Agnes, crossly.

"Perhaps you know this gentleman? He lives very near."

"Oh! Barker Preston?" exclaimed Agnes, with a return of liveliness. "Every one knows of him!"

"Mr. Preston! no, that is not it;" said Lord Englefield, looking a good deal more put out. Here was a fresh enemy. "No, I mean a Mr. Colville."

Agnes cast a withering glance on Lord Englefield. She drew herself up and looked proudly, almost fiercely at him, as she said, "And what of him? what does Mrs. Crofton dare to say of him?"

Lord Englefield looked surprised.

Agnes started, and said, warmly, "It makes me angry when I hear people gossipping of one another. You are surprised at my indignation, Lord Englefield, but when you know that Mr. Colville is a poor invalid recluse, you will not be so much astonished."

"Oh! really," said Lord Englefield, much relieved. "Mrs. Crofton spoke as if there was a sort of mystery, and I heard her say he frequently came and sat a long time with Miss Crofton, and, I think, meant to insinuate that they were not unlikely to......" He stopped suddenly, as he looked at Agnes, and exclaimed, "Miss Spencer, you are ill!"

"I do not feel very well," said Agnes. "It is that odious conservatory. I cannot bear the scent of some flowers."

"What shall I do for you?" said Lord Englefield, with all fitting civility.

"Oh! thank you, I am better again, but I will move away from these flowers;" and Agnes left the room. Lord Englefield had gained nothing, except that the dreaded Mr. Colville did not seem a very dangerous rival. Still Lucy, in her gentle way, repulsed him, and she was again as cold in her manner as civility would allow.

CHAPTER XXXIV.

"AFTER all," said Agnes Spencer one morning half to herself, half to Mr. Fairfax, "after all, I like Lord Englefield."

"If you left out the two first words," said Mr. Fairfax, drily, "Englefield would not be surprised. But, tell me, after all what?"

"The world tried so hard to spoil him, that I thought it had been successful," said Agnes; "but, the fact is, he is improved, as many men are, by falling in love."

"I agree with you. Englefield is *coming out*. I always liked him, and I always thought he would. The fair lady is Miss Crofton, I suppose."

"Yes," said Agnes, "and he would be a fortunate man if he succeeded."

"If he succeeded!" said Mr. Fairfax; "you don't mean that fifteen thousand a year, and a very good-looking, agreeable youth appended to it, would be rejected?"

"Indeed, I do," said Agnes.

"What will you bet upon it?" said Mr. Fairfax, smiling ironically. "I am ready to take any odds."

"Do you know Lucy Crofton?" asked Agnes.

"I see a pretty ladylike girl here, with no very distinctive characteristic about her......"

"Ah! I see you *do not* know Miss Crofton!" said Agnes; "but, while I nobly refuse your bet, remember, you are bound never to sneer at the disinterestedness of women again, if I am right."

"Done, Miss Spencer."

"Done," said Agnes, with a merry shake of her head. She sat down to write a letter: others of the party came in. Lucy seated herself near Agnes for protection from Lord Englefield; a little *coterie* of ladies, over whom Mrs. Digby presided, were deep in gossiping, and after various exclamations of "How extraordinary!" "Oh! dear, how delightful!" "Quite like a novel!" there was a general rush towards Lucy, with an eager request that she would tell them all about Mr. Colville. Mrs. Digby had been telling them that they had a real live hermit in their neighbourhood, and that he came to visit the Parsonage by stealth!

"We are dying to hear all that he says and

does, so pray tell us everything about him, Miss Crofton."

Agnes Spencer looked up from her writing with proud indignation kindling in her eye. Lord Englefield heard and saw, and watched with anxiety for the effect on Lucy. Mr. Fairfax, attracted by the noise of voices, looked with no slight ill-humour on the interruption to his studies, and also fixed his critical eye upon her; she was not aware of this alarming set of watchers, and she answered very simply and readily—

"I cannot tell you anything about Mr. Colville."

"Oh! Miss Crofton, why not? Why can't you?"

"As Mr. Colville wishes to live in retirement, we could not abuse the confidence he has placed in us, by making him the subject of gossip;" was Lucy's answer, with a quiet trust that the propriety of her refusal could not be doubted. Mr. Fairfax wheeled his chair nearer to Agnes.

"I withdraw my bet," he said in a low voice; "she is a noble lassie!" And Agnes, with a sparkling eye, gave a bright glance of approval first to him, and then to Lucy; and then, I was told, that her eyes filled with tears; and she was soon pacing up and down the broad gravel walk before the conservatory, as if fighting down her own emotion, whatever it might be.

Lord Englefield could also appreciate Lucy's delicacy of feeling, although it puzzled some of the party. Lady Frances exclaimed that she hated mysteries. Miss Crofton, with all her simplicity, was very deep.

When the ladies retired to their rooms at night, Agnes lingered with Lucy.

"What say you to the constancy of men in love? Do you believe in it?" was her sudden question, as if a new thought had struck her.

"It must depend on individual character, I should think," said Lucy; "and we could no more class all men together in this respect, than as to talent or temper, or any other characteristic."

"Then, you do think it possible?" said Agnes. She was speaking in a constrained manner, as if cross with Lucy, and yet determined to get her opinion.

"I have had no experience," said Lucy, faintly smiling. She hoped to escape a subject which was far more painful than Agnes could be at all aware of.

"Do you mean to accept Lord Englefield, and in all the pretty things that he can offer to you, forget the friends you have made at Hulse?" was her next question, and it seemed to account for her ill-humour. Agnes must have received the very false impression that she was encouraging Lord Englefield for the sake of his rank and wealth. Lucy answered warmly, for she was much hurt at such a suspicion from Agnes.

"I hope Lord Englefield will never offer them to me; and I am very sorry if my manner has seemed like encouragement," were her words.

"I spoke foolishly!" said Agnes, quickly. "Pray forgive me, Lucy. I never thought you wished Lord Englefield to propose, and nothing could be more perfect than your manner." And yet Agnes was not like herself. There was evidently something more she wished to say. "I utterly abhor all the missishness of young lady confidences," she said, "just as much as you can do; owing to this we are both of us ignorant of what may have been passing in one another's hearts all this time. Except indeed," she added gravely, "that you know my love has been, and is over for ever. But your life is beginning—your life of love, at any rate! and why am I to know nothing of it?"

There was something at this moment so perverse and strange about Agnes, that it is impossible to say whether she would have persevered in her half-taunting tone, had she known what acute pain she was causing to Lucy.

"I have grown up with a horror of such confidences," said Lucy; "one's own secret cannot be told, without betraying that of another, and I see no right any woman has to abuse the confidence that love alone has entrusted her with."

"What if you and I were to love the same person!" said Agnes, with increasing perversity. "Should we hate one another?" Her piercing eyes were fixed on Lucy. "It might be no fault of yours, and yet I might hate you."

"Let us think of nothing so dreadful," said Lucy, whilst a little shudder ran through her; "we have suffering enough without imagining impossible evils."

"Why impossible?" still persisted Agnes.

"Nay," said Lucy, with nervous hastiness, as if wearied out by Agnes's perseverance on a topic of such extreme trial to herself, "why will you persist in forcing from me what I do not wish to say? I love one with whom I know you are not in love. And now, Agnes, I have said more than enough. Pray let the subject drop for ever."

"Oh, Lucy!" said Agnes, after a few moment's silence, and tears were in her eyes, "How hard and cruel I have been! But you must try to forgive me! I did not mean to wound you, and you shall be spared in future. Do not fear me—whatever happens I will still love you!"

Lucy received the affectionate words of Agnes with emotion. She was overcome by what had passed, and her languid eyes and pale face told it. She could not say much, and Agnes left her.

During the remainder of the time at Digby Manor, Miss Spencer watched Lucy almost as a mother would watch a favourite child. Even in the midst of gay or careless talk, there was tenderness in her eyes and voice, the moment she looked at her; but something mournful always seemed mixed up with her anxions, affectionate interest.

END OF VOL I.

www.ingramcontent.com/pod-product-compliance
Lightning Source LLC
Chambersburg PA
CBHW032055220426
43664CB00008B/1008